FAYE CORNHILL is a busine~ ~~~~h +~ +h~ wedding industry. With
her signature mix of positivity

specialises in helping aspirationa
making it in the world of weddi
    Faye's career as a busines
experience as one of the UK's
Today, as well as working one-to
movers and shakers, Faye also runs The Wedding business club. ~..is
private members club has become a thriving community of wedding
professionals from all across the globe.

    Faye firmly believes that mindset is the foundation for any successful
business. Her followers praise her ability to inspire and energise and she is
commended by prominent figures in the industry for leading by example.

Find out more at www.fayecornhillcoaching.co.uk

I
Do

HOW TO SAY *YES* TO RUNNING A SUCCESSFUL
AND PROFITABLE WEDDING BUSINESS

Faye Cornhill

SilverWood

Published in 2020 by SilverWood Books

SilverWood Books Ltd
14 Small Street, Bristol, BS1 1DE, United Kingdom
www.silverwoodbooks.co.uk

ISBN 978-1-80042-015-1 (paperback)
ISBN 978-1-80042-046-5 (ebook)

British Library Cataloguing in Publication Data
A CIP catalogue record for this book is available from
the British Library

Page design and typesetting by SilverWood Books

Dedicated to Harry and Grace
May you live your lives courageously
and with love in your hearts

Contents

Acknowledgements

This book has been made possible with the help of some amazing people. Thank you to my wonderful family; Phil, Harry and Grace. Phil, I thank my lucky stars every day that I met you. Without you by my side, saying yes to my crazy ideas, life wouldn't be nearly as fun. Your unwavering belief in me helps me believe that anything is possible. You gave me Harry and Grace, our best ever achievements. With the three of you in my life, I am complete.

Thank you to every member of The Wedding Business Club. Your energy and commitment amazes me daily. Being the Captain of our ship makes me so happy and I love leading you all towards success.

Thank you Jessica Killingley for not letting me get away with lame excuses for not writing this book. Turns out you were absolutely right, I have plenty to say. Thank you for believing in me and for becoming a dear friend.

And, of course, thank *you* for buying this book. I hope that you will find what you need in these pages and that your business will grow and flourish.

Faye x

My Story

I always knew I was going to run a business. As a child in the playground I could often be found touting my latest product range; anything from personalised letterheads to bespoke shampoo (I was seriously ahead of the curve). I had a way with words and just loved the buzz of exchanging stuff for actual money. It felt like a game, and the winner got more pocket money. WHAT a game. WHAT a buzz.

Of course, I didn't stay seven years old forever; adult life eventually kicked in. I picked up (mostly wonderful) big girl responsibilities: children, a marriage, a mortgage and full-time employment. Those things can feel less like a game and slightly more like a burden when the chips are down.

The lure of running my own business never disappeared. Occasionally I would daydream about being a business owner. The fire for freedom and for creative control was always burning but slowly over time the fire fizzled out. The capacity of my conscious mind was full. Fun stuff like starting a business got shunted down the food chain. It became an idea that loitered in the back room of my brain; I always knew it was there but I didn't allow myself to think about it very often.

I wish I could tell you that I had a Jerry Maguire moment where I yelled 'Show me the money' and left the office with a grand and dramatic exit clutching the goldfish. The truth is that I find it hard to really pinpoint the moment I declared 'That's it, I'm starting a business.' What I am clear on, however, is how I got to that stage. Without a shadow of a doubt, I attribute much of my success to my personal response when faced with a series of 'go for it' moments. I can recall so many times when I reached a T-junction in my own mind. Left = play it safe, stick with what I know, take no risks. Right = go for it. 'Go for it' moments are a bit like Thelma and Louise tearing down the highway in the open top car knowing that at some point there is going to be a canyon, but doing it anyway. These moments will be crucial to your success and will help you truly believe that you *are* good enough and that everything you want to achieve *is* indeed possible.

If you're waiting for perfection you'll be waiting forever. Speak to any successful business owner and they will tell you that nothing ever has been or ever will be perfect. I see so many people hiding behind this as an excuse to get started. Along with 'I don't have the time' or 'I don't have the money' or 'I don't have the experience'. If you're willing to hide behind these excuses then honestly this book won't be able to help you. To create a successful business, you need to make a commitment to yourself. A commitment that you'll seek self-fulfilment NOT perfection.

When I first started my wedding photography business, I had no clue about anything. If I'm being absolutely honest with you, I couldn't even take a very good picture! I was at sub-ground zero. It's for this very reason that I know it's possible for you. I'm not superwoman, I didn't get a special passage to success, there was no knee-up option for me. I played the long game, took consistent action and stayed patient, all the while wholeheartedly believing in myself. Working in the wedding industry has been and continues to be one of the greatest privileges in my life. When I wake up in the morning, I feel excited, grateful and full of joy to actually call this my job. The buzz is akin to those days back in the school playground. Work feels like a game again.

The purpose of this book is to help you create *your* game. Think of yourself as the game designer. You create the board, you choose the players, you create your challenges and, of course, you make the rules. I'm going to show you how you can give yourself a fighting chance of success; I'm going to show you how taking imperfect action will improve your odds and I'm going to show you exactly how to create the life and business you really desire.

If you're reading this book, then I want you to commit to getting the most out of it. Use that reading time wisely. When there are exercises, do them. When I give you ideas to take your business forward, listen to them. My way isn't the *only* way but it IS the way that has worked for me and hundreds of my clients.

Life is short, but it's great. Maybe you're at a T-junction right now and you need to decide which way to go. Maybe this is YOUR 'go for it' moment.

So, buckle up and get ready to take a massive leap forward. I'm going to show you how to start and run a passion-led business in the wedding industry, and finally crack the code of how to make money doing the thing you love.

How to Get the Most from This Book

I take my responsibility as author of this book really seriously. I know it takes time to read everything I have to say, and I know that your time is precious. I get it, and I'm grateful that you are trusting me. So, in order for you to get the most from the time you invest in this book I have some golden rules for you to follow.

1. Face your fears

There will be moments (the famous T-junctions I mentioned earlier!) when running your business feels scary, and you'll have a choice. You can choose to run away, hide, take the easy option, shy away. That's your prerogative. But when you do that, you send a clear and very loud signal to your subconscious mind. You're telling yourself that you're not good enough, and after doing this for a while you will programme yourself to run from fear. Sure enough, this will have a huge knock-on effect on the success of your business. Face your fear and EVERYTHING changes. You want to know how to cultivate self-belief? You face your fears. Even though the signs may be there to stop, give up, don't risk it, you get those big girl (or boy!) pants on and you go for it! Regardless of the actual outcome, that feeling of being worth it will breed and cultivate such a wonderful sense of self-belief that before long you'll be addicted.

2. Choose positivity

If you haven't already met a mood hoover in the wedding industry, you will very soon. These people can be found almost everywhere. In Facebook groups, in networking meetings, at wedding fairs, on Instagram. There are some common signs to look for:

- They often talk about how the industry 'is dying'.

- They often talk about how the industry 'is saturated'.

- They can often be heard making judgements about their competitors' businesses.

- You may even hear them say things like 'How does she think she can get away with charging that much when she's only been doing it for a year?'

These people try to recruit mood-hoover armies, so be very aware of their recruitment tactics. Now I've brought your attention to these people, you will immediately be able to spot them. The most important protection tactic is to spot when they try to recruit you. They will continue to speak negative chatter until they see their rhetoric taking hold of their victims, they will feed you with negativity, they will talk about the threats to the industry and stir the emotion up until you are a hot mess. Be aware of these people and STAY CLEAR. They are not your friends and they will not help you grow your business.

3. Figure out your non-negotiables

One of the things I always have a little giggle about is when I hear someone saying that they are starting a business because they want more time with their family. I said that too and then in my first season ended up being away from my family 100 per cent of my weekends. Listen, I'm not playing down the fact that in the long term, running a successful business will offer you freedom, but at the beginning you are going to be pulled from pillar to post. It's likely that you are going to feel really uncomfortable

– like you have less time and that your life is infinitely more stressful. It's important from the outset to know what your non-negotiables are. These are the things that you are unwilling to sacrifice. This is usually time – either with your family or on your own. So, if Sunday mornings are baby swim lesson times and that's a highlight of your week, don't be offering this as an option for consultation times. You are not available at that time. Period. Yes, things need to be fluid, but don't give up all of the joy in your life to grow a business; you don't need to.

4. Automate and outsource

I remember being told to do this and thinking: 'That's for people who've been in business longer, with more money and tons more clients than I have'. Nope. No, siree. Nada. This is for people who are smart and want to grow their business in the most efficient way possible. Identify the areas of running and growing your business that bring you the most grief, or the things that you are just no good at and don't have the hunger or desire to get better at. Those are the things you need to outsource. Look at the parts of your day-to-day business operations that are laborious and that seem to eat your time. These are the areas we need a system for. A system doesn't have to be a fancy pants piece of software; it can be as basic as a workflow spreadsheet. I used one of these for years that literally told me every action I needed to take with a client after they paid their deposit. I used a simple traffic light system to indicate when a task was complete. I started this system because I kept on forgetting little pieces of the puzzle and I was becoming aware that all of my clients were receiving a different experience. This simple and free spreadsheet ensured that every client of mine received exactly the same service. It's never too early to automate and outsource. By the time you *need* to, it's too late.

5. Start before you're ready

After about eighteen months of running my wedding photography business I started flirting with the idea of leaving my full-time job. I kept setting myself ridiculous: 'When I do XYZ, I will leave my job,' type goals. I was like a crazy stressed donkey chasing the carrot and every day the carrot got further and further away. My husband just said to me one day: 'Faye, you will never be ready. Why don't you just go for it?' The rest is history. I did exactly that. I stopped existing in the 'what if' mentality and started allowing myself to connect with the opportunity. I backed myself 100 per cent. I knew that with the amount of passion I had for my business I would make it a success. OK so the numbers didn't *quite* add up on paper but boy I was ready. I had so much fire in my belly I just knew I could make it happen. Start before you're ready, because you'll never be ready. You'll never have enough money, you'll never have enough experience, you'll never have enough time. Stop waiting and start doing.

6. Be patient and consistent

In stark contrast to my rallying cry in point five, patience is an incredibly powerful attribute. I am not patient. In a queue I'm a nightmare – I get twitchy, I shuffle my feet, I check my watch a million times and have even been known to 'tut'. I am totally impatient. BUT I have learned the hard way that patience is a virtue when it comes to running a business in the wedding industry. There are pieces of the puzzle (and we will come to those) that require you to wait for them. Let me give you an example. I created a list in my first year of business of the venues I wanted to approach to be added to their preferred supplier lists. In my head I wanted it to be a quick and easy process. I wanted to make instant relationships. I wanted to call them up and – poof – be accepted on their lists just like that. It's a nice idea but a totally unrealistic expectation of how it actually works. I had to be patient. I had to cultivate my relationships and look for opportunities. Consistency is key. Running a business is exactly the same as staying healthy. You can't eat one healthy meal and become 'healthy'. You can't go to the gym and instantly become fit. It's a slow burn but a worthwhile one. There will be times when you feel like telling your social media schedule to go to hell, when your blog is the last place you want to dedicate any time. The people who continue to show up consistently are the people that reap the rewards.

7. Be kind and stop the judging

Be kind. It's pretty simple really but annoyingly easy to forget. Kindness is an incredible tool for navigating life. It just makes everything so much easier. And in my experience, the kinder I am, the more lucky I become. Just recently I gave a high-ticket coaching experience to a previous client of mine, for free. No strings, no reason, I just wanted to. I did it quietly without a fanfare; only she and I know. And you know what – two weeks later, I experienced exactly the same level of kindness from someone else to me. It's super easy: be kind and the world will be kind back. There is no room for judgement in my life. I'm not holier than thou. I have moments when I just feel like having a rant. But it gets me nowhere. None of us should be judging other people. Stay in your lane, concern yourself with your own business and you'll be amazed how much happier you will feel.

8. Dream your own dream

It's very tempting to watch other people and fall into the trap of dreaming their dreams, of following their aspirations, of wanting their clients. For a long time, I thought I needed to become someone else to be successful in my businesses. I once even tried to dress and look differently for a photoshoot because I thought that was how people 'expected' me to look. You will never ever find the true meaning of happiness if you are living someone else's dream. Be true to yourself, find your own spark, fuel the fire in *your* belly – not someone else's. Remember, this is *your* game, you're the one in charge here, make your own set of rules.

Be you, stand tall for your values, be the person you were put on this planet to be, and I promise your people will find you. And when they do, they will love you for being you. You will be the answer to their prayers.

9. Know your why

If you do not know your 'why' for running your business, I strongly recommend that you down tools and get clear on this now. It's simple – if your reason for all of the hard work you're putting into your business isn't compelling enough, you will give up. There, I said it. A human really has to want something to make it happen. Because it's not all rosy; you will have tough times. When the chips are down, it's your desire to achieve your 'why' that will keep you going. During the tough periods of running my business I find it so powerful to reconnect myself with *why* achieving my goals is so important. What will my outcome be? If I'm ever lacking in motivation, I just need to look at photos of my 'why' – my husband and children – and I'm immediately anchored back into the zone of focus and productivity.

10. Stop making excuses

I hear too many excuses and it makes me so sad. There are three that I tend to hear more than any others and I want to call these out before you can even bring them up. They are:

- **Time.** Please don't test me on this one. I have worked full time (managing a team and a multi-million-pound client portfolio) while growing, birthing and raising two children and building a business all at the same time. I know what a lack of time feels like. Was I willing to let that stop me? **No way.** It takes just five minutes each day to take one action that will move you and your business forward. I know that some people will have more time than others, and for some people things will happen faster. But if you're adhering to point number eight you'll not be concerned with how much time *other people* have – you'll be concerning yourself with taking action in the time you have available. Stop thinking it's got to happen in five minutes. Be patient, but **be consistent.** Please, please, please stop using time as an excuse for a lack of dedication. Reminder: I'm not Wonder Woman or any more talented or skilled than the next person, I just got out of my own way and used the time available to the best of my ability.

- **Money.** There are so many FREE things you can do to help build your business – networking, social media, volunteering, joining Facebook groups, asking your peers, watching and learning, YouTube. Stop making excuses and start being creative. Having said that, I want to be absolutely clear on this: at some point you will need to invest money into your business. FACT. You cannot and absolutely should not desire to build a business with no money. You're not the expert at everything – work with the experts and you'll get there faster and with significantly less stress; just don't let a lack of available funds stop you from even getting off the starting blocks. You're worth more than that.

- **Experience.** Everyone started somewhere. Everyone has had their 'Day One'. Every professional was once a beginner. Are you really willing to let your ego stand in the way of your success? Roll your sleeves up, learn, get yourself in a room with people who know and have achieved more than you, and absorb their ideas and their methods. And be prepared to make mistakes and to learn from those, too. If you're not willing to start at the bottom, being a business owner isn't for you.

These are the guiding principles I follow for my life and my business.

I want you to think about these rules as promises. In fact, embracing all that is wonderful about our beloved wedding industry, I want you to think of these as vows. Vows that you're making to me, so that in return I can help you reach your full potential in your business. So, with that in mind, please turn the page and complete the agreement.

Dearly beloved, we are gathered here today, in the presence of your fellow wedding business owners, to witness the joining together of _____ (insert your name) with _____ (insert your business name) in blissful union.

Repeat after me:
I recognise that growing a wildly successful and profitable business is exactly what the universe has destined for me and I take my responsibility fully and willingly.

I _____ (insert your name) solemnly swear that I will:

1. Face my fears

2. Choose positivity

3. Figure out my non-negotiables

4. Automate and outsource

5. Start before I'm ready

6. Be patient

7. Be consistent

8. Dream my own dream

9. Know my why

10. Stop making excuses

_____

(Signature)

Perfect – *now* you're ready for this book – let's go!

Part One

Mindset

I firmly believe that the most important place to start when you're building a business is mindset. You can have the most inspiring brand with the most slick business and marketing operations, but if you don't believe in yourself, your business will flop. Mindset should be your number one priority.

A Balancing Act

A really tricky part of running a business of any size is balance. I've already touched on this briefly but I really wanted to make a special mention of this here. Many people in the wedding industry have the desire to leave full-time employment because they want to spend more time with their family/at home/doing what they love, and then almost immediately they realise that they have less time and feel significantly more stressed when they're running their business full time. This can be unbelievably frustrating and leads to people quitting. That's not what I want for you.

Balance is hard to achieve. Some days you will feel like a pro juggler, some days you will feel like a huge disaster. These are not measures of your success, that's just the way it goes. The true way to gauge your success is to look at how you're shaping your life to accommodate everything that you want it to include.

I will dive into this a little later in the book, but having a schedule is my key tip for running a successful business that moves forward. Now, you might be wondering how creating a schedule has anything to do with mindset. For me it has *everything* to do with it. Mindset work isn't all about vision boards, big dreams and positive thinking. A huge part of it is squeezing the most juice out of the time you have available.

Having coached hundreds of people on this, I see every day that a lack of progress in their businesses is the reason people give up. And I also see that the reason people fail to move forward is because they are not setting themselves up for success.

I have coached many people over the years who seem to literally stand still. Same actions = same results. And the one thing they all had in common was that they were firefighting their 'to-do' list rather than proactively running a forward-moving business. Their working week looks something like this:

Wait for stuff to come up. Deal with it. Try like hell not to explode with stress.

This is not the proactive approach I recommend to you for running a successful, profitable and balanced business. You have to be way more efficient than this to expect any sort of success.

Firefighting is not a business strategy. You need to adopt a strategic, proactive approach. Here are my top tips for achieving this:

- Get clear on your goals.

- Focus on your 'Big Three' goals (more on this later).

- Take one piece of action every single day that moves you forward towards achieving these three goals.

- Create a timetable for each day/week/month.

The timetable is so important and incredibly underrated in our industry.

Work out the time that you have available each week. This might be as little as an hour here and an hour there – it might not be what you want and need to create your dream business, but it's what you have right now, and that is OK. There's no point in sabotaging your future success because you don't have the perfect setup *right now*. Use what time you have and know that starting before you are ready will take you a step closer to a future that allows you all the time in the world.

I create a schedule on a Sunday evening, every week without fail. I look at the family commitments I have and block those into my diary. I look at the personal self-care commitments I have and block those into my diary. These are non-negotiable. I don't flex on this. My family and my self-care come first.

Once you are clear on the time you have left, create a list of all the tasks you would like to achieve during that week. These are NOT jobs that you'd 'like to achieve one day'. Be very clear on this. These tasks are actions that are going to move you and your business forward in the direction of your aspirations and goals. When I write out this list each week, I ask myself that exact question. "Will these tasks move me and my business forward and get me closer to my goals?" and if the answer is no, they get bumped off. It really is that simple.

Ambitious people can struggle with this. When I was working full time and building my business on the side, I found myself hugely frustrated and impatient. I wanted to do ALL of the things yesterday. You have to work with the situation that you have and be realistic about what is possible. Burnout won't lead you to quicker results, and it'll lead you to giving up your business. Work with the parameters you have to achieve *your* business success on *your* terms. Acknowledging that other people are on a different journey will help you make peace with the timescales available to you.

So, starting today – why not try this new way of achieving balance?

Goal Setting

Why do you need to set goals?

When I first decided to go solo and build my first business, there was a major piece of the puzzle that was missing from my master plan. I'm going to tell you exactly what this was, and we will be doing some work to understand how you can avoid making the same mistakes I did at the start.

Focusing on this first, before you dive into the nuts and bolts of running your business, will save you hours, days and maybe even years. It might sound pretty basic to you, but I need you to trust me on this because it could totally change the course of your business and your life. Ready? Here we go.

You have to know what you want.

You need to set some goals.

Yes folks, it really is that easy.

When I decided to start my business, I went at a million miles an hour into the nitty gritty of the business. My corporate experience had programmed me to focus on this first. I was straight into website design, Facebook ads, wedding shows, styled shoots. Before long I was knee deep in 'running a business' but with very few paying customers. To be honest it felt pretty good, but it felt like I was constantly hustling. I was extraordinarily busy doing things that were actually not helping me. I had craved the 'business' for a long time and I was finally there, working as crazily as I thought I should be. The obvious and very clear problem was that I had no idea what I was trying to do. Yes, I knew that I wanted to be a wedding photographer, but that was the extent of my brief. And that's really not good enough if you'd like to make your business sustainable. Let me say this really early on: hustling is not a mark of success. If you're doing all of the things all of the time, regardless of how much money you're making, that isn't winning. If you're constantly sprinting towards an undefined finish line, that's not winning either. That's running on fear. Trust me, I've been there.

Fear will be your most frequented T-junction. There were phases of the early days in my business where I went there on a daily basis. Any limiting belief I had in my head would make itself known the second things weren't going well for me. And from there I would spiral out of control. Think of it a little bit like a game of snakes and ladders. You're plodding along every day, sometimes shooting up a ladder. But at any moment you can find a snake (fear) and before you know it you can be back at square one.

So why does knowing what you want from your business make it any easier? It's actually very simple. Would you get in a car without an idea of where you're going? Nope. Do you play a game without understanding the objective? Nope.

Your business is no different. If you don't understand where you're heading then you'll stand zero chance of actually getting there. I hear so many business owners telling me they haven't 'made it', and when I ask where 'it' is, they have no idea. So many people are measuring their success against nothing. Or even worse, against someone else's success. Do that and you'll always be losing, you're guaranteeing yourself a 100 per cent failure rate, and you and your business deserve better than that.

I understand why you might be doing this. You're scared of setting yourself goals, because once they exist, you actually have to try and hit them. Am I right?

But the thing is, if you are not willing to set yourself some goals, you will be slowing yourself down, maybe even bringing yourself to a standstill.

Let me tell you about my client Jo. She was running a very successful business and had been for almost five years. Things were OK, money was coming in and she had a good reputation. But for that whole five years, she felt like she was always an arm's reach away from where she wanted to be. When I started working with her, I asked her what her goals were and she didn't know. After talking it over I realised that she'd been waiting to see where she ended up, rather than proactively taking control of her destination. Because of this she felt like she was constantly chasing success. We switched this up and set some three-month, six-month, annual, five-year and ten-year goals. Sure enough, within three months she had smashed her annual goals! Yep, she went further in those three months than she had for the entire previous year of running her business! It wasn't because she was lazy or uncommitted – far from it – she just hadn't had a game plan. I truly believe that if Jo had worked in this way from day one in her business, she could have halved the time it took to get where she was.

Want to get yourself the kind of business rocket-booster that Jo had? The good news is that you're reading this book now and we're going to kick start this way of working. So, grab yourself a pen and paper and let's get to work.

How do you set goals?

Let's get this show on the road and set out your goals. These are the exact steps I teach my private clients and the same process I go through myself when I want to set my own goals.

It might be that you are resistant to doing this. If that's you, I want to ask you to trust the process and I want you to trust me. And when you achieve these goals, I want you to send me a message to celebrate because I promise you, it all starts here.

So, find yourself a quiet space (seriously, trying to do this while feeding the kids or cooking dinner is just not possible!) Prioritise some quiet time when you have space to think and feel.

Off we go.

1. Grab a piece of paper and write down everything you would like to achieve in your life in the next ten years. When I say everything, I mean *everything*. Let your imagination run wild in the aisles and jot down anything that comes to mind. Make it colourful, draw

pictures – go crazy. There is only one but very important rule with this exercise. You will need to stop your subconscious mind from forcing you to think about the 'how'. I don't want you sabotaging your own success before you've started. The moment you start saying "But I don't have a clue about how to achieve this" – you need to stop. You want to buy a massive new house? Write it down! You want to move to Australia? Write it down! I don't care about how you're going to do it. It's not important right now. This step is all about the FEELING. Excuses are not welcome during this process; doubts serve no purpose whatsoever. So, dream big my lovely – writing it all down as you go.

2. Next, I want you to pick out the goals you'd like to achieve in ten years and write 'ten' next to these.

3. I want you then to do the same with the goals you would like to achieve in the next five years and three years. Write a 'five' or a 'three' next to those.

4. This will mean that the items left on your list are the goals you'd like to achieve this year. From this list I'd then like you to pick your top three goals. I want these to be the ones that stir up that delightful concoction of exhilaration and fear when you think about them. Highlight them, star them, draw them out again on Post-it notes. These are your goals for the next twelve months. Are you excited?

5. Now it's time to start on your plan for how to achieve these three main goals. Don't panic – this plan will start in the most beautifully simplistic way. I want you to dedicate ONE action for each of these goals that will take you closer to making them a reality.

Top tip: It might be that you have no idea what the actions could/should be. In which case the first thing you might do is ask for help. Let's face it, if you're reading this book it's likely that you're on the lookout for tips, so stay tuned for a whole bunch of actions that will help you in achieving these goals.

I want you to become very familiar with your goals. I want them to go everywhere with you. Make a note of them and carry them with you in your handbag or wallet, write them on your noticeboard, save them as a screenshot on your phone, put them on a Post-it note on your mirror. If I meet you and ask you what your goals are, I want you to tell me confidently what they are. I want you to think about them when you wake up. I want you to think about them when you go to sleep. Living and breathing these three goals will stand you in much better stead for achieving them in the next year. You can do this!

Knowing your goals will also massively help with batting off distractions. When you're under the cosh and feel like you're spinning a thousand plates, I want you to prioritise the activities that will move you closer to your goals – everything else can wait. When you're overwhelmed, the best way out is to simply ask which of the tasks you are faced with will help you achieve your goal the fastest. Identify those and prioritise those actions, the rest can wait.

I see so many people running around in circles doing all of the things. Stop. This will not help you. And it certainly won't enable you to help others. Cut to the chase; look at the actions that will move you forward towards your goals and focus on those.

Understanding why these goals are important

The next but equally important part of goal setting is establishing your 'why'. I touched on this in the introduction but it's a really important concept and one that I need you to grasp.

So, what do I mean? I mean understanding *why* you are striving to achieve your desires. *Why is this important to you? Why are you working so hard? Why are you committing so much time? What does this opportunity mean to you?*

As I have already mentioned, I hear a lot of people telling me that they started their own business because they want more time with their family. Those of us who have started our businesses will know that at the beginning, quite the opposite can happen. You will be working long hours, and you'll be away from your family. You might even miss important events. All because you were working so hard to create a different future.

So why are you doing it? There has to be a compelling reason *why*. Otherwise it would be a whole lot easier to go and get a job and be paid a regular income from someone else.

I don't want that for me, I don't want it for you. But you have to know why.

Why?

Because when things aren't going so well (which *will* happen at some point!) it's your 'why' that gets you through. It's your 'why' that helps you drag yourself out of bed when you really don't feel like it. It's your 'why' that helps you say yes, even when you are scared.

My why is simple. I want to provide my children with as many opportunities to lead a full, abundant and adventurous life as possible. That's it.

So, when times are tough, when I feel like things aren't going well, it's this desire that helps me get back up again, dust myself off and GO FOR IT.

Spend some time working on your why. It'll be the most valuable thing you take with you into the future of your business.

An example is my client Sarah. Sarah is a hair and make-up artist who was in fact a nurse for fifteen years. She always loved hair and make-up but never had aspirations to work in this field. Until she got married and hated the way she looked. She vowed that no other woman should feel how she felt on that day and set about creating a business to ensure it didn't happen.

Understanding your limiting beliefs

The other important part of the equation is to understand what limiting beliefs are going to sabotage your success. In fact, it is highly likely that some of these are already stopping you from enjoying the fruits of your labours.

I know very well about limiting beliefs because I've carried several for many years. Probably none so big as the belief that I need to lose weight to be successful. Now before you jump in and tell me that I'm not overweight, I know. For years I've had a prickly relationship with my weight and in some form or another I have used it as an excuse to not go further. I would tell myself that to stand on a stage and teach people I needed to be thinner. I actually believed that to truly inspire people the scales needed to read a certain number. It's taken me years to shed this very heavy baggage (the belief, not the weight!) and I wish I could have found a way sooner because I feel so much lighter now. The irony with this belief is that I actually inspire people just the way I am. Loving myself, warts and all, has been the wonder tonic my business and my clients needed.

So now it's your turn. Taking ten minutes I want you to write all of the limiting beliefs that are stopping you from setting and sticking to your goals.

To get your creative juices flowing let me tell you some of the limiting beliefs my clients have told me:

- I'm too old.

- I'm too young.

- I'm too fat.

- I'm too thin.

- I'm too ugly.

- I'm too pretty.

- I'm not good enough.

- I'm not experienced enough.

- I'm too experienced.

- I'm not confident enough.

- Nobody will give me money to do this.

- I have been in the industry for too long.

- I haven't been in the industry for long enough.

Now it's your go! Grab a pen and paper and write down your limiting beliefs. Every single one of them, please. I know it's painful and this process may well bring up some emotions that you've desperately been trying to bury. But until you understand these, you're decreasing your chances of moving forward in your business. So, again, giving yourself time, space and quiet – write them all down.

Let me explain how limiting beliefs work.

Your subconscious mind is trying to protect you. Throughout your whole life you have been conditioned by your family, your friends, society, the media and your culture. We are conditioned to believe certain things, to feel certain things and to behave in a certain way.

The most powerful of all our human needs is to 'belong' or to 'be accepted' or to 'fit in' and we subconsciously attempt to do this by living up to all of the conditioning we've been exposed to.

So, if you were brought up in a family, a society or a culture that told you:

- You're not good enough.

- You'll never make enough money.

- You'll never be successful working for yourself.

- People like us don't start businesses.

- You need to work for someone else to make enough money to have a family.

- Working for yourself is scary.

- Greedy people make all the money.

Your subconscious mind is going to spend a considerable amount of time looking for evidence to back up your beliefs. It wants to protect you, so it will look for all the evidence to prove to you that you are right. Can you see the irony of this situation?

So, with your limiting beliefs in mind (which we know now are not *your* limiting beliefs – they belong to your family, your culture, society etc.) I want you to look at whether any of these are actually serving you. Because whether you think it's a good idea or not, you are using these limiting beliefs to prove to yourself that you are not good enough. Your mind is telling you, "No, no I cannot possibly do xyz because I'm not experienced/rich/pretty/thin enough". Isn't that just such a ridiculous concept?! Every single day you are looking for evidence that your limiting belief is valid enough to stop you from chasing your dreams.

So, grabbing that pen and paper again I want you to list all of the concrete evidence that proves these beliefs are 100 per cent true. Yeah, I know. Tough right. That is because they are all completely fictitious.

False

Evidence

Appearing

Real

Part of your development as a business owner needs to be your understanding of the way your mind works because when you do this, you can understand how to take back control of the way you think and the way you feel.

Nobody puts this better than Mahatma Gandhi:

"Your beliefs become your thoughts. Your thoughts become your words. Your words become your actions. Your actions become your habits. Your habits become your value., Your values become your destiny."

I know this can feel pretty full on. You wanted to start a wedding business and now here you are suddenly talking about human psychology. But let me be very clear. This will be the make or break of your business. Ignore this at your own risk.

I've worked with many wedding business owners who have *only* changed this part of their life and have gone on to transform their business completely. Take my client Heather for example. When she first came to me, she was a struggling wedding photographer, barely making ends meet and considering whether to give up and get a 'proper job'. We focused almost 100 per cent on her mindset and within six months, I got this message:

"I've been meaning to message for some time now, but I was almost scared to, because I couldn't believe that what I wanted to thank you for had come true.

Since your coaching, and reaping all you taught me to sow in my business, everything has blossomed.

I am now counting fifty-five weddings that I have booked for this year, and booking steadily into next year. Not only that, I'm looking at the first time in my life, earning what will be forecasted for the year, a six-figure business income (what?!?!?!).

I'm running into 'problems' like too many enquiries and I have to turn down clients because I am already booked on a regular basis. It's a strange new (and very exciting) normal that is happening right now."

I share this with you to show you that all of this was possible for Heather when she started to focus on her mindset. The ripple effect that this generated on her business, her relationships and her life was enormous and genuinely life changing. This is possible for you too.

Your Money Story

When it comes to mindset, money plays a huge part. In fact, your money mindset gets a section of this book, to give us the space to explore it in the depth it deserves.

The relationship you have with money has a huge impact on the success of your business. The way you think and feel about money and the way you act around money will be reflected in the way that your clients think and feel around money. I remember key moments in my life and business when I actively changed the story I was telling myself about money. Don't get me wrong, this wasn't always easy, but every time I did it I saw my business move forward in huge bounds. Getting a handle on your money mindset, and knowing your own personal money story is a vital part of running a profitable business with the potential for real growth.

So what's a money story?

Your money story is your own personal financial blueprint. It is a combination of thoughts, feelings, beliefs and behaviours you have around money. It consists primarily of the information or programming you received in your past, usually before the age of seven, and these thoughts are lodged deep within your subconscious mind.

Most of us blame external sources for the reason we don't make enough money. Stop for a moment and think about the conversations you have with your friends, your family, a partner or even your children about money. Have you ever blamed one of the following for the lack of financial abundance in your life?

Your boss
Your clients
Your lack of clients
Your competitors
The industry
The economy
Your landlord
The government?

I'm guessing at some point you will have; I know that I have. When I was studying for my A-levels I worked as a cleaner in some offices in my village. It was an amazing job. I was seventeen and could listen to my Walkman and boogie along to the music as I hoovered the offices. I was so grateful for that job. There was a phase, however, when I started to begrudge the people's offices that I was cleaning. I used to imagine their lives, their homes, the opportunities they had in life. I would make all sorts of assumptions about the type of people they were. I would assume that they didn't care about people like me, cleaning their offices. I assumed they were greedy, flashy, show-offs. I imagined their children and wondered whether they cleaned offices to make pocket money. I doubted it and it made me feel annoyed.

Why would I think this way?

Conditioning from society, conditioning from my family, conditioning from my friends, conditioning from my peers.

Until one day when this bubble was (thankfully) burst. One Christmas I found a card and a box of biscuits left for me by a man who worked in one of the offices. The card said that he was really grateful for the efforts I went to, to make his offices a clean and tidy place to work for him and his staff. He said that if I apply the same level of diligence to my study as I did to the way I cleaned their offices I would have a bright future. He said if I ever needed a job to come and talk to him.

Wow. Talk about a wake-up call!

But it shouldn't take this situation to educate me about my limiting belief. It shouldn't have taken one person's kindness to overcome my negative assumptions. Imagine if that had never happened and I'd carried that belief into my adulthood. Imagine what limitations that would have presented for me.

I strongly believe that if you want to change the fruits; you have to change the roots.

Starting today, you need to change the way you feel about money, the way you talk about money and the way you feel about wanting more money in your life.

For a long time, I felt anxious about money. I would focus on the lack, the scarcity, the what-if. And of course, that is exactly what I would experience more of. I found it hard to think ahead because I was so consumed by the here and now, the moment of scarcity that I existed in. It was like a mild panic over me all the time. That was my money story playing over and over in my head. My beliefs, thoughts and feelings about money were stopping me from existing in a forward thinking, opportunity-focused way.

A crucial thing to remember at this point is that you don't need to have experienced major hardship to be affected by the rhetoric of scarcity in your own head. My upbringing was safe and welcoming. We lived in a lovely semi-detached home, my dad worked full time and my mum worked part time to support the family. When my sister and I were old enough, my mum went back to full-time employment. My parents were always there to support us, and although there were many things we didn't have, we enjoyed nice things. We were by no means wealthy but I don't ever remember being subject to hardship.

Yet I've still grown up with a complicated relationship with money. It wasn't until I did this work that I realised I had many limiting beliefs around all things financial. Some of them included:

Money doesn't grow on trees.
Money makes people greedy.
Rich people care less than working class people.
People like me don't make lots of money.

I know what you're thinking when you read this. How could I grow up with these beliefs when I have just told you that I had a safe and comfortable childhood?

Children process what they hear before the age of seven as fact. So, if you hear someone say 'money doesn't grow on trees' when you're growing up, you will eventually believe this to be true. Maybe not consciously, but subconsciously it's going to get into your head and under your skin. This limiting belief will then manifest itself into your life and your business and will affect the way you think, feel and behave.

Nine times out of ten, when it comes to making decisions about your business, money will play a huge factor. I would love to tell you that you can build a business without spending a penny, but I would be lying. Many people in the industry are starting with limited or no funds and, while that is absolutely OK, at some point you will need to invest in your business. Doing the work behind understanding your money story will make this particular 'go for it' moment a lot easier.

Deciphering your money story

How do you understand your money story and ensure that it isn't going to hold you back? First of all, you need to get to grips with what your money story is. You need to take a look back at the language that was used around money when you were a child. You need to tune into the things you heard, saw and felt as a child and start to unravel how these might be affecting you in your life and business today.

Sometimes this exercise can be an emotional one, so give yourself the time and space to work through these questions.

1. Write down a list of all of the things you heard about money when you were growing up. Example: rich people are greedy; money doesn't grow on trees.

2. What did you see about money when you were a child? How did people behave around each other and towards money when you were a child? Example: did people argue about money around you?

3. How did you feel about money when you were a child? Example: did it feel exciting and expansive or a burden and out of reach?

4. How do you feel about money now?

5. How do you feel about competitors of yours who have made lots of money in their business? Do you feel excited for them or jealous?

6. How do you feel about people who have more money than you? Do you feel envious or does it motivate you to desire more?

7. How do rich people make you feel? Do you feel threatened? Or do they inspire you to strive for more?

8. How do you feel when you imagine yourself making all the money you desire? Does it seem unrealistic or aspirational?

9. What do you tell yourself about the possibility of making money in your business? Do you tell yourself that it's not possible? Or do you tell yourself that anything is possible?

Once you've started to write this out, you will probably start to realise the connection between some of the thoughts you have, the feelings you experience and the behaviour that you display.

Now is a great time to mention the relationship between your thoughts and actions. This is because, whether we believe it or not, your thoughts dictate your life. Your beliefs become your thoughts. Your thoughts shape your behaviour.

Examples

If you think that people will never pay you for your service, you will believe this to be true. This belief will shape your behaviour – you won't charge what you are worth, you will negotiate on price, you will allow people to ask for discounts.

If you think only greedy people make money, you will believe this to be true. This belief will shape your behaviour – you will feel bad asking clients to pay you, it will result in people defaulting on payments and will fulfil the belief that you are not worthy.

Can you see the vital role that your money story plays in the success of your business?

Take my client Charlie. Charlie grew up believing that money was very hard to come by; that she had to work her fingers to the bone to scrape by and that people like her would never make any more money than the family members before her. Charlie, although an incredibly talented wedding planner, was sabotaging her own success by carrying a very complicated money story.

To be able to make a change in her life, Charlie first needed to understand her financial blueprint. She took the time to look back and unpick what she had heard, felt and understood about money growing up. We worked on disassociating with these beliefs and forming new ones.

In just twelve weeks, Charlie went from being nervous and suspicious around money to focused and driven. She went from apologising when she asked clients to pay, to confidently and assertively asking for payment. This in turn had a huge knock-on effect on her business. Her clients were valuing her time and creativity. She became increasingly confident about being visible and ultimately ended up raising her prices.

Charlie's story is like so many others I hear about money. Your beliefs around money can stop you before you've even get started, as well as prevent you from ever making a go of building a successful business.

Take a moment to write out what you are starting to notice about the relationship between your money story and your life. Awareness of your feelings towards money is a huge step towards changing your relationship with it for the better. Understanding how the story has formed from other people's beliefs will help you start to heal the negative emotions you associate with money.

The next stage is to take the time you need to understand how this story has unfolded for you over the years, disconnect from it and reprogram yourself to move past these limiting beliefs. Disassociating with the feelings that you have carried for a long time and which no longer serve you are very important to achieving a healthier money mindset.

Start by asking yourself whether the beliefs you have around money are true. Go back through the list of thoughts you have around money and put a * next to the thoughts that are factually correct. I expect there won't be many, if any at all. So, ask yourself how these beliefs are currently serving you. What role are they fulfilling in your life right now? That's right, there is no purpose. Next time you catch yourself thinking something that you know is not true, remind yourself of this fact and, if you can, repeat this exercise.

Since starting to work on my own personal money mindset I find that mantras are really important. Mantras are positive statements to read and repeat over and over. I have them on my phone, as the wallpaper on my laptop and on Post-it notes around my house and office. I have listed some below for you to help to reprogram yourself with a new story – one that's based on your truths and your new beliefs around what is possible.

Anything is possible.
I am worthy.
I am enough.
Money comes to those who believe in themselves.
Everything I desire is totally within my reach.
I am building a business that will bring me joy and financial abundance.

Changing your money mindset is not an overnight job, but it doesn't have to be a lifelong mission either. It all starts with the decision to change. In my experience of coaching hundreds of business owners over many years, I can say that the people who experience success all have one thing in common:
They make their success non-negotiable.
If you are serious about creating a sustainable and wildly profitable business, this work needs to become non-negotiable for you too.

Your money mindset evolution

Your money mindset evolution is likely to develop in a few stages:

1. Understanding your triggers

I want you to think about the things/people/situations in your life that trigger a negative response towards money. Maybe keep a little journal over the coming weeks to make a note of when you start to experience negative feelings. It might be that having certain conversations with certain people can set you off. It might be that doing your accounts can trigger you. It might be that you are so overwhelmed by even going near a spreadsheet that you avoid your accounts all year round, in anticipation of a mad end-of-financial-year panic. This is your opportunity to work out what your triggers are, who they are, when they show up and the way you feel in their presence. How exactly do you feel? Powerless, stupid, overwhelmed, confused, sad, worried?

2. Outsourcing

The next stage is really to think about what elements of these triggers can be removed from your life. I'm all for working through triggers and finding a coping mechanism (see next point) but I'm also a realist. Running a wedding business results in you wearing multiple hats and I believe that sometimes we need reminding that we are not experts in every single field. If you're building a wedding business it doesn't mean you're a web developer or a social media manager or an accountant. I was late to start working with an accountant but the second I did I realised what a life-changing move this was. I was treading water with my accounts and was on the brink of sinking at any moment. Don't do this to yourself. The first year I filed a tax return with the help of my accountant she actually saved me £500. This paid for her bill and gave me some money in my back pocket.

3. Working through the triggers

Not everything can be outsourced and certainly not everything *should* be outsourced. No matter how deeply rooted your aversion to spreadsheets and numbers is, you need to find a way to make friends with your numbers. You are the captain of your ship and you need to know how this thing sails. If you are working with an accountant, they will be able to help you create a simple cashflow spreadsheet. If you're working without an accountant this is something that you can set up yourself and that will serve you really well as your business moves forward. I recommend keeping it SIMPLE.

If your trigger is a certain person or a certain conversation it's time for you to take control. Perhaps a friend or family member has a strong opinion about money which triggers you. Starting right now, make yourself unavailable for this conversation (politely and respectfully, of course). It might even be worth explaining that you're working on your money mindset and you'd really appreciate not having those conversations anymore. People are so much more sensitive to mental health now and should respect your preferences. If it's a certain person that continually triggers you, avoid them if you are able to. I know it seems full on, but

I truly believe that when you're building a business you need to be very picky about who you spend your time with. Be around open-minded people who see the opportunity that life brings. Make yourself unavailable for anyone else.

4. Making it a daily focus

Like I said, money mindset work is not an overnight job. It takes time, it takes practice and there will be bumps in the road ahead. I've dedicated more than ten years to my mindset work and I'm not there yet because mindset isn't a destination, it's a journey. There are no finishers' medals. You'll know when you're winning because the way you react will start to change. Previous situations that would have triggered you become less and less dangerous. Your mind is a muscle and you need to tone it. Make a note of situations that you managed better; even a small difference is a win and means you're on the path to taking control of your thoughts. And when you have control of your thoughts, you have control over your feelings, and when you have that you will be able to change your behaviour.

I read all the time. It's a bit of a joke in our house because my husband will be on holiday reading a novel or a biography of a sports person. I'll be perched on the sun lounger with a business book and a stack of Post-it notes. Someone called me 'obsessed' once, which I thought was funny, because it suggests that there is something to be ashamed of. I'm not ashamed at all of the years of work I've put into making myself think, feel and behave in a way that is congruent with my values. For years, talking about money was like a constant toothache. Now it's an abundant conversation that makes me feel full of opportunity. I might look a bit bonkers on the sun lounger but it's a risk I'm willing to take.

I try not to promise things, I'm a coach, not a genie. But I promise you that, if you show up and do this work, it *will* change your life and your business.

Mindset Summary

Before moving onto the next section of this book I want you to ensure that you have:

- Set your goals for the next year.

- Understood exactly why these are important to you and your business.

- Written out and started to work on removing your limiting beliefs.

- Written down and reflected upon your money story.

Book Bonuses

I've created a library of resources that are yours for free. Come over to www.fayecornhillcoaching.co.uk/bookbonuses where you'll find:

1. A weekly planner
2. Social media mantra graphics
3. Cashflow spreadsheet template
4. Two meditations

Part Two

Branding

A beautiful and captivating brand grants you access to communicate with, and book, clients who love what you do. There are key things to consider which are often overlooked, in this section we dive deep into understanding exactly how to create a brand that acts as a magnet to your ideal clients.

Your Ideal Clients

In this chapter we are going to talk about why understanding who your ideal clients are is so important. I want to kick off by dropping a really important truth bomb! Because a question I get asked all the time is 'Why do I need to know who my ideal client is? Can't I just work with anyone who is willing to pay me?'

#TRUTHBOMB
If you try to attract everyone to your business you will end up attracting nobody.

Let's imagine you really need to buy an apple. You're on the high street and there are two shops. One is an apple shop and the other one is a supermarket. Which one would you go in? You'd go to the apple shop because you know they sell what you need. It's likely that the supermarket sells apples but you know that there is a chance you might leave empty handed.

Think about it. When you walk down the high street or when you're shopping online, what makes you stop? What makes you interested in a shop window? What makes you physically go into a shop? Take a moment to think about a time when a shop has attracted you from the outside and turned out to be perfect for you inside. What was it called? What was the colour scheme? What did its signage look like? What was in the window? What could you see from the outside? Who were the other shoppers in there? When you went inside, how did it make you feel? Were you greeted and if so, how? How was everything laid out? What was the decor like?

All of these elements of your casual shopping trip will have been perfectly curated to create an overall experience that was attractive to you (i.e. the ideal client of that particular brand). This is exactly what you need to do for *your* ideal clients. But just to be crystal clear, I want to address the often-asked question of 'why can't you have a shop that attracts everyone?'

Aside from struggling to attract the right clients, being a 'jack-of-all-trades' is a sure-fire way to feel truly dissatisfied with your work. It means you will struggle to get the right content for your website and social media, it will almost guarantee that you will have to fight for clients and you will constantly be asked to negotiate on price. Do you want to work like this? No, I didn't think so. So many people assume that it's the price of their business that is wrong when so often it's the demographic of the clients that they are attracting that needs to be changed.

Having a clear idea of your ideal client means that your clients will choose you based on *your* personality and *your* style, which is so important in the wedding industry. You want clients who will trust you and be guided by your experience and your creativity. Working with these clients will result in you having plenty of beautiful images to showcase your abilities on your website and social media. This is self-fulfilling because it will help you attract more ideal clients – and so the cycle will continue. It will result in you feeling a true connection with your clients and will mean that you build relationships based on style rather than price. When you work with ideal clients, they will respect your time and creativity, which in turn feeds the joy you have for the work you do, and inspires you to hit even greater heights. Would you rather work like this? Yep, thought so. So, let's get to work.

Before we dive head first into creating an ideal-client profile, I want you to think about this: to make money in the wedding industry (and indeed *any* industry) you need to help your potential clients fix their problems. I know what you're thinking, "I'm a wedding supplier, my clients don't have problems, they are getting married!" and this is a common misconception. Just because someone is planning a wonderful, pretty and exciting life event, it doesn't mean that they aren't scared, nervous or apprehensive. Admittedly sometimes these 'problems' can be pretty mild ones but nonetheless it's incredibly important that you are facilitating a way to solve them. Usually as a wedding supplier we are helping clients in one of these areas:

- A lack of time.

- A lack of creativity.

- A desire to look and feel good.

- A desire to create a unique and memorable event.

So, I want you to think about the following:

> Why does your ideal client *need* to book you?
> What will happen if your client *doesn't* book you?
> What makes *you* the best and only option for them?
> What is it about your story and your background that's going to resonate with them?

Getting clear on who your ideal client is will be a huge part of your future success. It will shape every single element of your business including your branding, your website, the words you use to describe yourself and your services, what you post on social media (more on that later!) and so much more.

So now that you have a really good understanding of this, let's shape it into a sentence that you can use going forward. For years I had this written on a scrap of paper on my noticeboard. Whenever I was having a wobble about a particular client or a decision I needed to make, I would always refer back to this.

Complete the following and fill in the blanks:

My target clients are (who are they?). Before they found me, they were (struggling/anxious/worried/uninspired etc). By choosing me as their (what you do) they will (what do they want?).

Here is an example I helped my client Lola create for her London based bridal boutique:

My target clients are fashion-driven modern brides. Before they found me, they were feeling disillusioned by the traditional wedding gowns they were seeing in high street shops and wondered whether they would ever find something to suit them and their contemporary style. By finding their dream gown in our studio they feel confident that their gown (and their wedding!) will reflect their passion for fashion and wow their guests.

I recommend printing your version of this out, having it visible and using it to check back in whenever you feel confused about the shape of your brand or whether a particular client is right for you.

Think of this as your fairy dust, your unique magic potion. So many wedding suppliers are missing a trick by skipping this step, and it's a part of your business I really want you to focus on right now.

How to understand who your ideal client is

Now we know what your own particular brand of fairy dust is, we need to start thinking about building your ideal-client profile. This work is relevant for everyone reading this book. Whether you are just starting out or twenty years into running a business, this work is crucial to your success and should not be overlooked. Indeed, your ideal-client profile will evolve over time and should be something you revisit as and when you feel like your brand changes direction.

Before you skip ahead and start reading all of the questions, I want to make something really clear for you. It's OK if you don't know the answer. It's OK if the profile you build here does not reflect the clients you are booking right now. It's OK if you have no idea how to attract them. For now, I want you to leave all of your 'what ifs' to one side and just get stuck into the idea of choosing the type of clients you want to book.

1. Are they male/female, same-sex couple?

2. How old are they?

3. What are their jobs?

4. What are their salaries? And how much disposable income do they have?

5. Where do they live? Where do they work? Where were they brought up?

6. What religion are they?

7. Do they have children?

8. What is their house like?

9. Who do they live with? Do they live together?

10. Do they own their house?

11. What is their relationship like with their home? Do they love interiors?

12. What's the best part of their home?

13. What do they do at home – family time, entertaining, work?

14. What are some of their likes and dislikes?

15. What hobbies do they have?

16. Where do they go in their down time? Who do they go with?

17. What's their favourite restaurant?

18. Where do they go on holiday? What's their dream holiday?

19. What do they read?

20. What's their favourite shop? What do they enjoy spending money on?

21. What sort of clothes do they wear?

22. Who is their style icon?

23. What do they like doing together?

24. How do they spend weekends?

25. Are they on social media? Which one(s)?

26. What is their wedding budget?

27. Where are they getting married?

28. How would they describe the style of their wedding?

29. Who is involved in the planning?

30. Who is the dress designer?

31. Where is the honeymoon?

32. Where is the gift list?

33. What is the most important thing about their wedding?

34. What are their challenges with wedding planning?

35. What will they be like on their wedding day?

36. What makes them your kind of person?

37. What won't their wedding be like?

Hopefully by completing this, you've got a better understanding of the type of client you would like to attract for your business. To reiterate, please don't waste your time right now focusing on the fact that you don't know *how* to attract them. Use your time now to zone in on understanding *who they are*. We will talk about how to attract them when we get to the marketing chapter. Don't worry. I've got you covered.

OK, we've touched on aspects of this already but it's vital now to do a deep dive on the wedding itself in order to best understand how you can help them (and to get further clarity on the sorts of weddings you want to work *on*, not only the sort of clients you want to work *with*).

You don't *need* every wedding. You don't *need* every client. So, let's get super focused on the people you really *want*.

I want you to think. Is your ideal clients' wedding:

>Traditional? Modern?
>Religious? Alternative? Church? Temple? Mosque? Civil?
>Village hall? Mansion house? Palace? Beach? Barn?
>Creative? Simple? Detail-driven? Luxury? Budget?
>Stylish? Simple?
>Colourful? Monotone? Bright? Pastel?

A really good way to start building a picture of what sort of weddings you would like to work on is to create a Pinterest board. Remember not to get caught up in the 'how will I actually book these weddings?' for now – just let yourself flow with your creativity and create a board of the weddings that make you happy, make you feel inspired and that you aspire to be involved with.

If you've never used Pinterest, it's super simple and absolutely brilliant. Head over there and set up an account (it's free!). Create a board (call it something like 'Ideal Client Inspiration') and use the search box at the top to type in words that you have circled above. When you find pictures or content that you like, click on the red pin button and save it to your ideal-client-inspiration board. Think of using Pinterest as a quicker way to make a mood board – and one that uses much less paper and glue stick!

Don't underestimate how useful this exercise can be. I did this again a few years back when I was approaching a rebrand and even though I was many years into running a successful wedding photography business, I realised from this one exercise alone that my style, my look, my edit and my overall brand had changed a lot. Brands evolve; styles change, and creating a Pinterest board can really help you keep track of this. It is also hugely helpful for creating a brand that speaks volumes to your ideal client. We will come to this shortly.

For now, go and pin to your heart's content, and when you're done, take a moment to check for consistency between everything we have covered in this chapter. Go back to the questions you answered at the beginning about who your ideal client is, look at the descriptions of their weddings, look at your ideal client statement. Do these add up to everything you are seeing on the Pinterest board you have created? If so, I think you're onto a winner!

Does your brand attract your ideal client?

You might be wondering what on earth you do with this new ideal-client avatar that you have created. It looks great on your Pinterest board but how do you actually translate it into moving your business forward?

Now it's your opportunity to start looking at everything about your business to see whether it is currently in line with your ideal-client profile. I call this a brand audit. If you're at the very early stages of running a wedding business, you might be tempted to jump past this stage. I wouldn't advise that you do this – the information I'm about to share with you is invaluable to attracting your dream clients.

So, let's start with conducting an audit of your business to understand whether the brand that you currently have is attracting and converting your ideal client.

Let me be clear, PLEASE DO NOT PANIC IF IT'S NOT! The way I have structured this book is to cover all of the super important parts of your business and to support you in the transition if necessary. The critical work for you to do is around understanding who your ideal client is and what is currently not evidencing this message in your business.

So, I want you to take an audit of your business attributes and conclude how well they are speaking to and attracting your ideal client. These include:

Your brand (including logo, colour palette, fonts, textures and patterns).
Your website.
The copy on your website.
The imagery on your website.
Any marketing material/brochures.
Social media channels.

Spend some time comparing the ideal-client profile you have created in this chapter and zooming in on your business attributes (as listed above) to look for any clashes. It's likely there will be a disconnect somewhere, and it's your next job to bridge that gap (please don't panic, I will be telling you exactly how to do that!)

So, here are some questions for you to ask:

- Does your brand/logo have similarities with the brands that your ideal client is already buying?

- Does the colour scheme/pattern/font choice reflect the design preferences of your ideal client?

- Does your website offer the sort of experience your ideal client is seeking from a wedding supplier?

- Does the text on your website speak directly to your ideal client and use the sort of language that they find appealing?

- Does your brochure look and feel like the sort of quality your ideal client looks for?

- Are you showing up on social media in a way that resonates with the problems/worries/concerns of your ideal client during their wedding planning?

When I do this exercise with people, I usually get the response 'I don't know' which is OK. You might *not* know. But this part of this process is going to involve you making aspirational decisions. You call the shots, and you make the choice when it comes to the sort of clients you want to attract. So, if you don't feel like you know the answers, it's time to make some decisions and commit to the direction of your business.

Research is always so important and so underrated. Part of moving away from thinking about your business as a hobby and treating it like an actual business is…well…actually running it like a business! All successful businesses will be spending time and money on research. The good news for you is that you can do this bit of market research with very little time and no budget.

If you're yet to actually work with any clients that's fine. This is still really important work for you to do as soon as you have booked your first client. Always follow these steps to understand each and every booking that you make in your business. It will help you shape the future of your branding and marketing strategy.

So, for those of you who have worked with real clients I want you to go away and speak to the ones who fit your ideal-client profile. I want you to ask them the following questions:

- Where did you find out about me?

- What was it about me that made you decide I was the right choice for your wedding?

- What was it about my service that made you decide I was right for your wedding?

- Is there anything you would have changed about the contact/booking/service process that I provided?

- Is there anything in particular that you really liked about the contact/booking/service process that I provided?

This feedback is gold dust – it's your key to unlocking more of your ideal clients! I want you to add this feedback gathering process to your workflow. Never consider a job complete until you have requested feedback. Sometimes you won't get the feedback you thought you'd get or wanted to get. Sometimes you might even disagree, but overall, you will be getting amazing information from your ideal clients which will help you shape an even more powerful brand message.

Lastly on this subject and before we move onto your brand itself, I have one more task I'd like you to complete. I want you to write yourself a testimonial. I love this exercise because it highlights the often-forgotten fact that you get to choose who your clients are. If you follow my methods you won't run a business that gets whichever clients come your way. No, you will attract clients who you *choose*. And the writing of your own testimonial is an important piece of this puzzle.

My wedding photographer client Kate, did this very exercise and here's what she said about it.

"When Faye asked me to write my own testimonial the idea seemed crazy. I was still in the mindset of thinking I would take money from anyone who wanted to pay me. It was so liberating to suddenly have the power to choose the people I want to work with and represented a huge shift in my mindset. I wrote a glowing testimonial from my ideal client and printed it off and framed it by my desk. I held the vision of working with this client for a long time and this really helped me gain clarity in so many areas of my business. Then finally, FINALLY, I got an actual testimonial from my ideal client that was even better than the one I had written myself. That moment was an absolute milestone in my business and I remember messaging Faye to tell her that, after all those months I finally understood the lesson."

So, I want you to imagine you just got your BEST ever testimonial. Write it JUST as your ideal client would.

- What does it say?
- Who was it written by?

- What are they praising you for?

- What was it about you that particularly attracted them to you?

- What was it about your way of working that they enjoyed so much?

When you're done, print it, save it, copy it and read it often – just as Kate did. Use it to motivate yourself when you're feeling low, use it as a tool to focus on your goals and visualise your future. Knowing that one day soon you will be able to replace this testimonial with a real one from your ideal client should be a wonderful motivator for you.

Your Brand

Now I want to look specifically at your brand and why it is such an important piece of the puzzle when it comes to attracting your ideal client. Over the years I have rebranded several times and will, of course, rebrand again at some point. A brand is never a fixed thing, it's a moveable concept that must grow and develop with you and the group of clients you are looking to attract to your business.

When I first started my business, I was on a budget, as I'm sure many of you reading this are. I got a friend to make a logo for me and my brief was this: "I'd like it to be black and pink." That was it. No mention of the client I was trying to attract, nothing of the message I was trying to portray. And although my friend created a logo that was absolutely *fine* at that time (and, I'll be honest, I was over the moon with it – it was like seeing my name in lights!) it did precisely nothing to attract my ideal clients. Mainly because I didn't realise that I needed to be doing that. So just by reading this book and understanding this concept you are already a million miles ahead of where I was.

Now I'm by no means painting a picture of disaster. That logo (it wasn't a brand; it was basically just a font choice) carried me through a couple of years of running a nice little business. I made money and

I enjoyed what I was doing. But I now know that I could have taken a shortcut. And that shortcut would have been understanding who my ideal client was and creating a fully realised *brand* that spoke to them. The wedding business owners I work with now are achieving what I did in a matter of weeks and months when it took me several years. A strong brand can catapult you towards success. Don't do what I did. The shortcut is right there, take it!

I want to make one thing absolutely clear at this stage. Your brand is not your logo. Yes, your logo is one of the elements of your brand but it's only one part. There is so much more to a successful wedding industry brand. If you can get all of these elements into one consistent brand you will be onto a winner!

Go back to the idea of youself walking down the high street. Remind yourself of which shop entices you and, once you're inside, what the experience you have looks and feels like.

So, with that in mind, let's have a think about the elements that make up a successful wedding business:

1. your brand persona,

2. your brand elements,

3. your brand promise.

1. Your brand persona

Every brand has a persona. When I think of a brand, I see it as a person. I can think of any brand, close my eyes and imagine what they would be like. I imagine how they would sound, I imagine the type of things they would say, I imagine what they would wear, where they would shop, what they eat, where they go on holiday and their favourite restaurant. If you go back to your ideal-client profile in the last chapter you will remember covering all of these elements. Now is your time to start creating a brand that has a personality. This way your ideal clients will really feel as though they are making a friend when they come into contact with it.

If this still feels a little bit far-fetched, I'd like to invite you to think about two brands that do the same thing, but attract a different group of clients. Let's say Ben and Jerrys and Haagen Daaz. Take a moment to think about the persona of each of these brands – if they were both a person, what would they be like? And perhaps most importantly, who would you rather go to dinner with? Why?

Ready to try it for your own brand?

2. Your brand elements

The elements of your brand will include all of its visual assets – your logo, your website, your colour scheme, your patterns and your packaging. I love brand elements and get very excited every time a client of mine creates a suite of them that's consistent and clear. The way these elements work together is the most important part. Think about a brand whose elements are always consistent. Apple is a really good example of this. There is a reason that they are one of the biggest companies in the world and it's not just down to their amazing technology. If you've ever bought an Apple product, you'll have experienced and unboxed one of their products – the experience is always the same and never gets any less exciting.

Wedding photography clients of mine responded incredibly well to my suite of consistent brand elements when I first created them. As well as having a strong brand and website I would send cards in the post, I would send little gifts and branded emails. Every single one of these touch points cultivated their loyalty, bit by bit. When I finally delivered their wedding photos, I would package up my branded USB stick and send it in a branded box with personalised tissue paper. The response was always magical. It can take you from looking and feeling like a small-fry business owner to owning your position as a true professional in your field.

3. Your brand promise

I love this element of a brand and yet it's one that I see people missing all of the time. Think of the John Lewis promise – Never Knowingly Undersold. They promise you that they will never knowingly charge you more than they should. The promise breeds a sense of trust and respect. Or the Tesco promise of 'Every Little Helps'. The promise is that they are trying to help their shoppers – little by little. Think about how you can communicate your brand promise across your brand elements. Maybe it's communicated through the copy on your website, maybe it's a strapline or indeed it may just be the way you are showing up for your clients.

With these three elements in mind I want you to start carving out the way your brand looks and feels. By now you know exactly who your ideal client is, so this is your opportunity to create a brand that speaks volumes to these people.

Creating a beautiful brand

Creating a compelling brand has to be one of the biggest sticking points I see wedding business owners experiencing. The truth is that you can be the most talented photographer/make-up artist/florist etc, but if you don't have a beautiful brand that creates a platform for people to experience your talent, you will remain hidden for a long time. You're going to make it much harder for yourself.

For a long time, I wrongly assumed that people would only be attracted to my actual work – the pictures of weddings that I was photographing. But I know now that I was wrong. It takes more than that to convert someone from being a distant admirer to an actual paying customer. An amazing brand gives your work a platform to stand on, a platform that raises you above even your own expectations and throws a spotlight on you and your talent.

In short, a good brand is essential to your success.

The good news is that you have a couple of options when it comes to creating your brand and I'm going to run through each of these options so that you can work out your best course of action.

- Design it yourself/ask a friend.
- Buy a premade logo/brand.
- Invest in a full branding service.

Design it yourself/ask a friend

Designing my own brand was never an option for me because I just didn't have a clue where to start. While I would happily describe myself as a creative person, I'd never claim to be an expert in brand design. It's something sufficiently far out of my wheel house to guarantee it a place on my 'to outsource' list! I know there are many very talented people in my community though, so if you would relish the idea of creating a brand yourself and you're confident that you can create something amazing, go for it! I would recommend using the following strategy:

1. Create a Pinterest board to spark the foundation of what works well for you and your ideal client.

2. Consider all of the elements needed for your brand. You will definitely need: a logo, a colour palette, a selection of fonts and design elements (such as textures and patterns).

3. Use professional design software such as Adobe Illustrator or Photoshop. Having full design control over your brand is essential. You need the flexibility to be able to use it as and when you need to for your website and your social media. I wouldn't recommend creating brands in software such as Canva. I love Canva as a programme for creating social media graphics but not for a full brand design.

4. Create multiple versions of your brand. It's really useful to be able to compare colour schemes and patterns to see clearly what really works for you. Give yourself some options rather than just creating one.

5. If you are asking a friend to work on this with you, I would encourage them to work to the above steps. Be clear with them on the timescales that you are working towards and set completion dates for each stage. Working with a friend can be an amazing experience but you need a mutual agreement on turnaround timescales and expectations.

Buy a premade logo/brand

There is a huge market for off-the-shelf premade logos. In fact, after my 'black and pink' logo, my next logo was a premade logo I bought on Etsy for $20. There are hundreds of graphic designers offering these and also basic branding services on sites like Etsy, People per hour, 99designs and Creative Market. I've seen some really lovely brands come from these and if you are on a tight budget for your business this is definitely a good place to start.

Please try to avoid the trap that I fell into though, which is believing that a logo was a brand. It's not. It takes more than a nice font to create a compelling brand. So please, if you're going to follow this route, make sure you are considering all of the other elements of what makes up an amazing brand. Don't forget, branding isn't vanity. It's there to purposefully attract and convert your ideal clients, and it's part of your business model that shouldn't be taken lightly. Try not to fall into the trap of creating a logo that looks like everyone else's. Remember, you should be focused on creating a brand that really chimes with your ideal client.

Invest in a full branding service

The absolute best option for your business will be outsourcing the creation of your brand to a design expert. This eliminates any of the stress behind creating the look, style and feel of your brand and designing your brand elements. As I've already mentioned, I'm a huge advocate in choosing the path of least resistance. When it comes to branding, if your budget will allow it, I wholeheartedly recommend investing in a branding expert.

Choose carefully though. There are lots of designers out there. The wedding industry is special and unique for many reasons and I do believe finding someone who has experience of creating compelling wedding brands is really important. Look at the previous work of a designer – are their brands and designs speaking to you? Do you connect with the designer on a personal level? Do they understand the wedding industry? Speak with the designer face to face (online counts!) and work out whether they have a thorough understanding of you and your business.

My underlying message here is that if you have the budget and you are committed to creating this business for the long term, outsourcing the creation of your brand to a professional is 100 per cent the right way to go. If you don't have the budget *yet*, that's fine too. Just make sure you are considering all of the brand elements and either creating or buying an off-the-shelf option that reflects your brand persona as best it can.

Should you rebrand?

If you already have a brand you might be reading this and wondering if now is the right time to change things up with a rebrand. There are no hard and fast rules about this, and I see it as a pretty simple decision really. If you have done all of the work around your ideal client and you are confident that your brand is on point with them and representing your brand persona to its fullest potential, then no – you don't *need* to rebrand. Maybe you could take the time to look through your brand elements and establish whether there is anything you could be doing that would improve what you already have. Maybe you just need to tweak the colour palette slightly? Simple and subtle changes can often reap big rewards.

If, however, you've done the ideal-client work and you're feeling uninspired and flat about your brand, I would say this is definitely a sign that change is due. To recap, your brand is a moveable thing – it will continue to evolve and change, and making sure that you keep up with it is an important obligation of being a business owner. Don't be disheartened by this, try to see it as a chance to hone your brand into something that's really going to represent where you are now and all the potential that your business has. It's an exciting opportunity to really connect with your ideal clients.

Your Website

Now, we are going to look into why having a great website is such an important part of your business. Previously I mentioned that when I first started out, I asked my friend to create a brand based on it being 'pink and black'. At the same time, I also sent this same friend a screenshot of a website I liked the look of and told my friend I wanted 'something like this'.

I was falling into the same trap as I did with my branding. I wasn't looking at the clients I wanted to convert and creating an experience for them, I was just looking at the successful photographers around me and assuming I had to be like them. The second mistake with my website was that I couldn't edit it. My friend built my website on a platform that I had zero clues about. I kid you not, to add a single image into my gallery took me about an hour and every time I did it, I actually forgot the process and got myself in a real flap. The outcome of this was that I avoided updating my website, it was filled with old imagery that I didn't love anymore, and I just didn't enjoy being around the website as a whole. This is not what you should be doing.

A website is your shop window (unless of course you also have a physical shop – in which case it's your *pre*-shop window). It has a huge opportunity to entice your potential clients, wow them and then convert them to paying clients. Never underestimate the power of an amazing website, it can truly change your business.

I have spent many hours studying the decision making and buying habits of wedding couples and although it differs from couple to couple, most people follow the same pattern. It goes something like this:

- Decide you need to hire a photographer/florist/make-up artist etc.

- Google photographer/florist/make-up artist etc. *or* ask friend for a recommendation.

- Look at their website.

- Seek social proof (i.e. check them out on social media).

- Go back to their website.

- Go back again to their website.

- Have another look at their website.

- Fill in the contact form to get a brochure or pricing details.

Time and time again it's this process that people follow. Your website tends to be the place that people go back to time and time again. Yes, they also check out your social media presence, but it's the website that is the make or break of an enquiry. (Of course, after the enquiry stage there is a whole process that will need to kick in to convert that enquiry to an actual booking, but never fear – we'll go into detail on this in the Business section). For now, we are looking specifically at what a website should be doing to get people to that point.

Your website has several jobs:

1. To showcase your work.

2. To tell your prospective clients about why you are the best choice for them.

3. To manage their expectation of working with you.

4. To facilitate the next stage of conversation.

1. To showcase your work

I have already said that my website was so overwhelming that I never changed the imagery. I want to stress again – this is not conducive to running a successful business. Your website absolutely must show your best work and the work that you would like to undertake again. If you've been involved in a wedding and the result wasn't something you want to do again, do not show these pictures on your website. I see websites every day with hundreds and hundreds of pictures showing a huge range of different looks, feels and themes. Remember what we said about this when we were looking specifically at your ideal client? Only show what that client wants to see, everything else can go. It takes multiple great images to convert a client and just one bad image to turn them off. Many people believe that when it comes to imagery the more equals the merrier, which I wholeheartedly disagree with. If you are already up and running with your business, do yourself a favour now and go back through your website deleting anything and everything that doesn't bring you joy anymore.

2. To tell your prospective clients about why you are the best choice for them

A crucial thing to remember is that you are the heart of your website, not just the services you provide. I see so many websites that have no mention of the business owner. If there is no picture and/or a mention of you and what you do and why you're the best choice for a client on your homepage, go and make this happen. The wedding industry is based on relationships. It is just as important that they love you as it is that they love your work. It is important to be offering a solution to their problem. Are you doing this on your website? If not, now is the time to change that.

3. To manage their expectation of working with you

When I first started my wedding photography business, I was trying to be everything to everyone. If my clients wanted me to shoot in a certain way I'd say yes and jump right in. Even if it wasn't really something I wanted to do. I thought and hoped this would make me seem keen and eager and would help boost my credibility. Unfortunately, all this really did was overstretch me and flatten my creativity. I remember agreeing to colour pop (remember colour popping?!) a bride's bouquet on a whole series of images. I wanted to cry tears of frustration and, quite frankly, embarrassment. I prayed she didn't tag me on social media in case anyone saw these images I had agreed to create for her. I don't want that for you. On your website you need to spell it out with unflinching clarity exactly what you do and how you do it. Leave no areas of doubt over exactly who you are. Yes, this will repel some people, but that's no bad thing! It will deepen your ideal clients' desire to work with you.

4. To facilitate the next stage of conversation

As important as a website is, the overriding purpose of one is to get your prospective clients to the next stage of the relationship – sending you an enquiry. A good website offers people multiple opportunities to get in touch, to request a brochure, to arrange a call. These 'invitations' are called calls to action (CTAs) and should appear on every single page of your website. Human behaviour is simple when it comes to reading a website – give people an opportunity to move their relationship with you forward, and they will. It's a bit like the chocolate bars at the tills in supermarkets. Oh, go on then, I'll have one. As soon as I added CTAs to every page of my website my enquiry rate skyrocketed.

What do I need on my website?

So, what's the magic formula for an outstanding website? I believe there are some 'must-have' pages that people expect to see when they visit your website. Of course, websites evolve all the time but at the time of writing this book, these are the pages I would recommend you include at a minimum:

- Homepage
- About Me
- Gallery
- How I work
- Pricing

- FAQ
- Contact
- Blog

Homepage

Your homepage is the most important page to get right, and if the stats are true then you literally have a matter of seconds to make the desired impact. I believe a good homepage has several jobs. It needs to loudly and clearly speak your brand persona and values, it needs to tell people exactly what you do, and it needs to transport your reader to their next desired destination. Clear signposting is absolutely necessary for your homepage. I see lots of people coming up with fancy ideas to design things differently but I'm pretty old school. I like a clear and simple menu bar that allows me to quickly decide where to go next. I don't want to have to search for things, you know I'm all about the path of least resistance. I also love it when I see a bold positioning statement on the homepage. This is usually in large font and the first sentence I see on the homepage. Ideally in this sentence you will encapsulate what you do and who you do it for. For example, on my coaching website I have this: "I inspire, motivate and energise creative business owners to build profitable and wildly successful businesses."

About Me page

Your about me page has one purpose – to tell people why they like you. So, thinking about your ideal client, tune into exactly what it is about you, your background, your life and the way you work that is perfect for them. Whether you like it or not, we need to see a picture of you, too. This picture should be shot by a professional photographer and needs to be 100 per cent on-brand. Think about your brand colour palette, think about your persona and work with a photographer who can incorporate this into one shot. Never underestimate how important this single picture is.

Gallery

Regardless of what you sell people, we need to see pictures. The wedding industry is a very visual one and people need to see what you do in order to make a connection with your product and/or service. These pictures need to be of professional quality. I understand that this is challenging when you are not a photographer but it's essential for you to have this to convert high-quality leads. If you're a photographer this isn't going to be a problem for you, but just remember that you must show only your best work. If you're anyone else and perhaps not a dab hand with a camera, you need to find a way to be able to include high-quality shots of your work. The first and most obvious way is to network with photographers who have shot weddings that you have been involved with. Most good photographers will be open and willing to share their work with you in return for crediting them. Aside from this, or in the event that you haven't actually worked on any weddings yet, it's your responsibility to work with a professional to provide you with credible photos of your work. A styled shoot can also incorporate photos of you and will offer a full suite of pictures for use on your website and your social media. In my opinion (and it's not just because I'm a photographer!) imagery can make or break a website as much as branding can.

How I work

Some people choose to include this information on their homepage, some include it on their about me page – it's up to you to figure out how and where this works best for you. But it really is something I wouldn't miss out on. Put yourself in the shoes of someone getting married for the first time – it's highly likely that they have never booked a cake maker/ florist etc. What might seem obvious to you about your service will be completely new to some of your clients. Be the supplier that is helpful, that offers tangible and useful resources and information to help them make their decision. If you're a cake maker, for example, some guidance on how many portions or how many tiers people need to feed x number of guests is *really* useful information that other cake makers take for granted. Additionally, everyone will have their own booking procedure. What is this procedure? Manage your clients' expectations so that they can get excited about being under your guidance.

Pricing

Ah, the age-old question: "Should I include pricing on my website?" This is a black and white question for me – 100 per cent I believe that the answer is yes. I personally find it so frustrating to visit a website, feel excited about their service or product to be told the only way of understanding their pricing is to send an enquiry. I don't need the ins and outs of every package detail but I do need at a very minimum a start price, or a 'my clients usually spend an average of £x'. In the absence of a price on your website, your visitors will make an assumption – they might assume you're too expensive or indeed that you are too cheap. Either way this isn't the best way to go about attracting enquiries. Including pricing detail also saves you time because it will deter the bargain hunters. It's not a good use of time, nor does it feel good, getting enquiries from people whose only motivation is to negotiate the lowest price possible.

FAQs

I love an FAQ section/page and if you find that your potential clients usually ask a similar collection of questions then an FAQ page acts as a really useful way of a) overcoming any possible objections and b) saving you valuable time going back and forth answering them on emails. In my experience I find that if I am covering off the obvious questions with an FAQ page, by the time I actually get to speak with or meet up with potential clients, we can focus more on our relationship, on building a meaningful connection and on getting mutually excited about their event than the ins and outs of the more transactional stuff.

Contact

You need to facilitate some sort of page that is dedicated to them contacting you. My personal preference for this is to have a contact form which prompts people with a series of questions for them to answer. This means that you are getting all of the information that you need to deal with the enquiry and also creates a lovely atmosphere in which you take each other seriously. I would avoid having a contact page that offers just an email address and/or phone number. In this day and age, fewer and fewer people choose to pick up the phone to make their initial enquiry, and offering an email means they have to copy and paste it into their email system. A contact form makes it easy for them. I would ask for their names, their date, their venue (unless you are a venue!), their ideas for the look/style/theme of the wedding and, very importantly, how they heard about you. We will come to this in the business section, but measuring the source of your enquiries is SO important. I would recommend linking this contact form to an automated mail system. There are many options available but popular ones are Mailchimp or MailerLite. As soon as someone completes the contact form on my photography website two things happen:

1. They are taken to a page which tells them what will happen next. I explain that an automated email will be waiting for them in their inbox with a copy of my full pricing brochure. I also tell them that within 24 hours I will check my availability for their wedding date and will send another follow up email.

2. I show them an online digital version of my brochure for them to see immediately.

This process means that usually I am the only photographer to offer them immediate access to my brochure and I'm already in their inbox ready and waiting.

Blog

Whether you love blogging or loathe it, it's something you need to have and do. Blogs work in two ways. They are a useful source of information for your prospective clients and they help you get found on Google. Your website must have a blog and I strongly recommend that you blog regularly. Be realistic about what is manageable for you and your lifestyle – consistency is more important than frequency. So, if weekly blogs feel a bit suffocating, go for fortnightly. Just make sure that they are published regularly – at the same day and time. In the marketing section of this book we will talk more about copy and the importance of keywords on your website and blog posts.

How to create an awesome website

So hopefully by now you understand the importance of having a good website and you're starting to see how you can build one that reflects your brand identity. I understand the stress that can be involved in building your own website though and if this is something that is stopping you from taking action then I would like to run through a couple of options.

1. Design it yourself

Designing your own website is easier now that it has ever been before. When I built my first website, 'templates' didn't exist. If you wanted to build your own website you needed to buy a copy of *Coding for Dummies* and after several stressful weeks and months you might come out the other side with something that sort of resembled a website. I am so relieved for you (and for me) that those days are gone! These days we are blessed with so many amazing ways to quickly and efficiently build ourselves a website. My personal preference for website design is WordPress because of its flexibility and variety of options.

If you're going to use WordPress I recommend using Divi as the platform to build your pages. It's a superb piece of software that enables you to build your pages visually with easy drag and drop options.

Using WordPress and Divi I recommend that you buy a template, often called a 'theme'. These templates offer you an 'off-the shelf' website that is super simple to drop in your brand/colour palette/patterns textures' and quickly and efficiently create a beautiful website.

2. Outsourcing

If the idea of creating your website makes you shudder and it's not something you have the time or inclination for, it's time to outsource. This was an obvious choice for me because I knew that I didn't have the time available to create the impact I wanted. Find someone who will work with you and will not only build a site for you but will help you learn how to use and edit the site. Learn from my mistake – not being able to make simple changes will be a thorn in your side.

Your website shouldn't be something you rush and won't be something that happens overnight, but getting it right can be the start of something huge for you.

Brand Summary

Before moving onto the next section of this book I want you to ensure that you:

- Understand exactly who your ideal client is.

- Understand whether your current brand is attracting and converting that ideal client.

- Have created your brand persona, brand elements and brand promise.

- Have decided whether you need to rebrand and if so the best route for you.

- Have decided exactly how you are going to create a website to reflect your brand.

Book Bonuses

I've created a library of resources that are yours for free. Come over to www.fayecornhillcoaching.co.uk/bookbonuses where you'll find:

1. An ideal-client map
2. A brand audit process

Part Three

Marketing

This is where the wheels fall off for so many people. There just seem to be so many options and such little time. In this section we are going deep into understanding exactly how to attract and convert those potential clients to bookings.

Creative Copywriting

We are now going to look at why the words you use are so important, and I'll give you some guidelines on exactly what you need to do to create compelling copy that reflects your brand and connects with your clients. Because copy is key I think it's possibly the most forgotten part of a wedding business, yet it's *so* important. I massively underestimated the power of words when I started my wedding business. In actual fact I didn't even *have* any words on the homepage of my website. I thought that because we worked in such a visual industry, coupled with the fact that I was a photographer meant it was all about the images. And while of course imagery is important, the copy you use on your website, your social media and also throughout the communication you have with your clients is an absolutely critical part of your success.

I wanted to start with covering off the fact that I really struggle writing about myself too, and I am sure many of you feel the same way. If you're anything like me you will struggle to say nice things about yourself and your work. I find writing 'about me' page content for someone else so easy, and in fact rather enjoyable, but when it comes to writing it for myself, I get sweaty palms and clam up.

My good friend and copywriter Jen Feroze of Jackdaw Editorial often tells me that we are all storytellers. I know, I know, I can hear you giggling right now, at the notion that you are a storyteller. But it's true and she's absolutely right. We all have a story to tell and it's a really important part of why a potential client will become a paying client. Words have the ability to set the scene, to manage client expectations and to ultimately persuade someone to hire you.

So where do we start? For me it was very much about coming to terms with the fact that I absolutely needed good copy on my website, on my social media and throughout the conversations I have with my clients and prospective clients. As soon as I could *understand* the importance of this I could willingly sit and write.

So, if you don't yet understand the importance of good copy let's start with a little experiment to help you get there. I want you to think of two or three brands that you love. Brands that you might have thought about during the ideal client chapter. I want you to think of brands that you feel really speak to you and encourage you to buy from them. I want you to take a moment to visit their websites and read their social media captions. Perhaps you could even subscribe to their newsletters and read exactly how they communicate with their audience.

I want you to consciously read their copy and highlight words they use and the brand persona they display. It might be that you are drawn to a particular brand because of the opulence of their luxury products. Maybe it's the simplicity of a brand that you find really relatable and you like the way they keep their copy on-brand with this. Check in with their choice of language and the words they use.

I'll give you an example. A shop that is guaranteed to entice me off the high street is The White Company. The brand hits a spot for me because I love the clean aesthetics, I like their minimalist window displays and I appreciate the muted tones of their products. Aside from this when I visit their website, they use language that I enjoy. They talk about 'Blissful Bed Linens'. That works for me because I want my sleep to be blissful and I prefer the choice of the word 'linens' over covers. It makes them seem better quality with an edge of luxury. Their diffusers have the most wonderful scene-setting descriptions that again, completely speak to me. They use words such as windswept, timeless, comfort, ozonic and evocative. I'm all in when I read this because it paints a picture that I enjoy creating in my own head. It sets a scene and it's a scene I very much want to be a part of.

Now you might be thinking this all seems a little bit over the top, but I promise you it absolutely is not. You are selling to someone who is planning the best day of their lives – the one day that people work for months and in some cases *years* towards. Choosing you is a BIG DEAL, never underestimate this.

The persona, and therefore the connotation of the language you use, is so very important. So, again taking The White Company as an example, they talk in a very casual way. They talk about 'cosying up on the sofa' or 'lazing back in a bath overflowing with bubbles'. This language says to me that it's a friendly and casual but luxury business. If I read their website and then went to their shop my expectation is not to be served caviar and champagne upon arrival (perhaps I would read copy like this on the website of Rolex instead) but I would expect to be greeted with a friendly smile from a smart, on-trend woman who has great style.

So hopefully by now I have converted the most sceptical of you to the view that copy does deserve your time and focus. When someone re-writes their website copy it can result in a huge shift. Not just for you and the way you feel about your website but very much for your prospective clients, the likelihood of booking you and the expectations you set with your clients.

Next up we are going to break down the areas for you to focus on when it comes to your wording, and give you some of the tools you need to start writing captivating copy for your clients.

How to write copy that converts

The first step towards writing copy that converts is deciding on a flavour and tone that mirrors you, your work and your brand. When all of these things add up, magic really does happen.

I found a really useful place to start with this was a word bank. In fact, when I did this, I actually dug out my school thesaurus (presented to me by my favourite primary school teacher, Mrs Axten *c.*1991). I used my branding Pinterest board and came up with some words that described what I was seeing in those pictures. I then did the same with examples of my wedding photography and added more words to the list to describe what I saw in those. This exercise was truly invaluable and one I really want to encourage you to do now.

Please don't get fixated on how 'good' these words are – we can find more appropriate versions of words that hit the spot (using my trusty 1991 thesaurus!) Just let whatever comes up for you go down on the page.

My list included these for my wedding photography brand:

Love
Family
Unique
Special
Memories
Bond
Organic
Simple
Warm
Natural
Cherished

If you go and have a look at my wedding photography website (www. fayecornhillphotography.co.uk) you will hopefully see how I have crafted my website copy to use these, and how the copy I have written reflects the work I produce and is in keeping with my brand.

From here I was able to decide what I wanted the persona of my copy to be. Looking at my word bank and my work I decided on the concept of 'laid-back luxury' which made it so much easier for me to write copy for the website and social media. I wanted to use my copy to create a picture of how people could expect me to be. I want them to know that I am confident and experienced, and that I create breathtaking photography that will move people to tears. I want my clients to know that I have photographed weddings at some of Europe's most amazing venues but that my favourite thing to photograph is, very simply, love. I want them to know that I'm quite happy to kick off my shoes and get on that dance floor if it means that I get the best shot. That is the persona I want people to experience when they visit my website.

So please, take this time to make your own word bank and create your own persona for your website. As tempting as it might be, please don't rush this process.

When you've done this and you are armed with your word bank

and your persona, the next stage is to actually start creating copy for your prospective clients to read. Let's have an honest think about the chunks of copy you need for your business. Of course, as your business grows and evolves there will be more, but for most wedding businesses the key areas for you to focus on are

1. Website (the pages and sections discussed in the previous chapter).

2. Your social media captions.

3. Your client communication.

1. Website

This can feel like the most overwhelming piece of the puzzle which is why it's where I like to start first. Your home page is the best and most impactful place to make an impression through your copy. With these words (which I recommend to be at least 300) it's your opportunity to tell people who you are, what you do, why you do it and how you do it in such a unique way. If you do this using your bank of words and reflecting your brand persona you will create the best possible first impression for someone who lands on your website.

Also, on your website is your about me page. This can be the most cringey one to write and I know that many of you will already be breaking out into a sweat just thinking about it. But I'm going to take you back to Jen's belief that we are all storytellers. You might be looking around thinking that everyone has a 'better' or 'more interesting' story than you. That is totally subjective. Your ideal clients will want to hear *your* story, I promise you. I hid behind my brand and my website for a good few years. I was scared of judgement and suffered massively from imposter syndrome. Hiding doesn't cure this. The antidote is doing the work.

So, start off by just writing. Yep, grab a pen and paper or start typing and just write. About you, your work, your aspirations, your craft. Just *write*. This first attempt will almost certainly not end up on your website. In fact, tell yourself – this is NOT for my website, I'm just going to write. Release the energy block that is stopping you and just let those words flow. If you do this and commit to the process fully you will end up with something that feels honest, sincere and that sounds like *you*. This is the perfect starting point that you can then go ahead and polish up to eventually use on your website.

2. Social media captions

Ooooh, have I had a love/hate relationship with social media captions? I've tried every possible equation for getting this right and my findings are that your most successful captions are ones that you write from the heart. I went through a super lazy phase of writing things like 'Look at this beautiful wedding bouquet' which at the time seemed like a quick and easy way to get the job done. On reflection it feels like a wasted opportunity to connect with my potential clients because let's be honest, who can connect with that? Yes, they might love the composition and edit of the picture, and the actual flowers themselves but nobody falls in love with that caption. I wasn't using any words from my bank and I wasn't portraying my brand persona whatsoever.

We'll be covering this in more detail when we talk about social media (yep, it'll propel your brand forward so much that it's got its own section of the book). Sometimes I just can't muster the magic to write in this way, so I wait until I can. I always feel massively inspired when I walk my dog so I'll often record voice notes so that I can write them up when I get home. Work out the trigger for your caption writing creativity and make it into a process.

3. Your client communication

The way you speak to your clients from the very start will have a huge effect on the way they perceive you, how much they respect you, how much they bond with you and what their expectations of you and your product/service will be. From that very first email, it's imperative that you are using words from your word bank and building a consistent picture of the brand persona they have seen on your website and social media. For me it's very much about being confident and displaying my experience (so that people know I'm a safe pair of hands) but also talking about my aspirations for the weddings I photograph. If the tone and the language I use don't hit the spot for a prospective client it's likely they won't want to further the relationship. And that is OK. I want to further relationships with people who understand my brand and choose to work with someone like me, and this is the attitude you need to start cultivating, too.

I hope these pointers have got your creative juices flowing. So, before you read any further, give it a go. Grab a piece of paper and a pen and just *write*.

I understand that not everyone is going to want to write their own copy and indeed not everyone has the time to write their own copy and that is absolutely fine. Outsourcing the writing of your copy to a professional is a completely legitimate thing to do. My advice is to choose wisely. The wedding industry is unique, so working with someone who has experience of it will definitely mean you get a different result. The good news is there's a talented pool of professional copywriters out there who specialise in creative, wedding and lifestyle brands and businesses, so make sure you do your research and find someone who understands you and the goal you're trying to achieve.

Networking

Networking feels like a taboo word for some people. It can leave them feeling overwhelmed and make them cringe. Lots of my clients assume that networking means asking people for favours, seeking approval and trying to make people like you. This couldn't be further from the truth.

When I worked in the corporate world I had to go to 'networking' meetings. They were terrible. The room was full of much older men wearing grey suits and clasping clipboards. Each member of the group had to speak out loud for a few minutes and I distinctly remember looking around the room as I watched these people chest puff. It was certainly not the rising tide community I was looking for. Even though it was billed as an event to help and support, it was more about 'he who shouts the loudest'. After a series of rather awkward meetings and over-the-top hard handshaking I decided this was not the place for me. These were not people I aspired to be like or spend more time with. If that has also been your experience of networking, let me reassure you that this is absolutely not what I want for you. Networking in the wedding industry is a very different opportunity.

By its very definition, networking means to connect and interact with others. There's no implication of asking for anything in return, seeking approval or even asking for an endorsement. As humans, we network with people every day. I wonder how many of you know about the life of your hairdresser or have chatted over the fence to a neighbour about their plans for a summer holiday. If you can do that, it'll be incredibly easy to engage with industry friends who care passionately about your work. The quicker you realise just how easy networking is, the quicker you can let this massively effective tool into your life and start making money.

Networking helped me catapult my business to success very quickly. I wanted to target 'luxury' clients (clients who will pay my higher prices!) and by growing my network with other luxury businesses I did this in a very short space of time. Of course, this shift was also reliant on me having the right brand and website (and indeed everything else we've talked about so far), but the icing on the cake was my ability to get out there and find my tribe.

If you are feeling nervous about this, let me offer some comfort and say that I was utterly terrified of doing this. I've mentioned already in the book about the first wedding show I attended. The photographer I was really inspired by was there, much to my horror/excitement. I had spent many hours fawning over her website and wondering if I could ever be as good as her. Now she was there, about fifteen feet from me, with her incredibly pretty stand and high-quality wedding albums. I experienced all of the emotions that day, not least because I'd just had a baby and was barely capable of leaving the house – let alone exhibiting at a wedding show.

I'm so grateful to myself on that day for having the courage to go and say hello to her. I wish I could go back and hug myself and say "go girl" for having the guts to do that. Because actually that one decision opened up a hundred different avenues. We became friends (which still sounds funny to say, I held her in such high regard it was like making friends with a celebrity) and I went on to meet so many other amazingly lovely and talented people. We even gave each other referrals when we were already booked and leaned on each other for advice during the tough times.

If you only take one thing from networking, let it be this: never assume that other suppliers are better/more confident/not interested/ above you/too experienced/have enough friends. I absolutely promise you that the people at the top of the tree feel just the same as the people starting out. Even when I got to the stage of charging £5,000 for a wedding, I *still* had moments of feeling like a fraud. I still do now. Success doesn't make you invincible and success certainly doesn't mean you don't still need friends.

Community is so incredibly important to the success of your business. That's why I set up The Wedding Business Club. Aside from all of the teaching I offer, I wanted to create a community where people were encouraged and inspired by other people. As we know, the wedding industry is unique, and speaking to your family members, your non-industry friends and even your spouse/partner about it can be tough. I have a wonderfully supportive husband and family but at times they didn't know about the sacrifices I needed to make to get my business off the ground. They didn't understand the lengths to which I needed to go to make sure I was keeping up with my aspirations. Surrounding yourself with people who have been, or are, in the same boat as you will be the biggest leap forward you take.

Networking with people who were ahead of me in their journey suddenly became a really aspirational experience for me, and not something that triggered my imposter syndrome anymore. I enjoyed lapping up the knowledge, the wisdom and the learning from other people's experiences (as well as their mistakes).

I genuinely believe that if you want to go far in this industry this is one aspect of running your business you just cannot afford to ignore. It's just so important. Not just for the growth of your business, but also for the growth in your confidence.

I believe with all my heart that a rising tide lifts all boats.

Your networking strategy

So how are you going to do this? Time for some tips that will make this process easier for you, allowing you to start creating a powerful network from today.

Follow and engage

This is an obvious one, yet I see so many people not doing it. We're lucky to be running our businesses in such a social time and space. Social media makes it incredibly easy to research, find and interact with people instantly. If you're not already following people in your industry (and importantly your competitors) then start now. If there are people, just like I met at that wedding show, whose work you find aspirational – follow them. Tell them that you think they are great. The 1980s way of running a business is not the twenty-first century way. You don't need to avoid other people and feel threatened by their success, you can choose to be inspired by them. Forgive this expression, but by *sliding into someone's DMs* you will automatically be a step closer to adding that person to your network.

Socialise

This one is pretty self-explanatory! If you want to connect with people there is no better way than asking if they would like to meet up and have a chat over a coffee. Yes, I know what you're thinking – "That sounds scary". It may very well be, but who said that building a successful business wasn't going to involve you doing scary things? The moment you step out of your comfort zone, take a look around. It's like a whole new universe – this is your learning zone and it's an incredibly fun place to be.

Don't assume that other people wouldn't be interested in meeting up with you. Don't assume that you're not good enough. I hear your concerns, I know it feels like a bold move, but I promise you that it will pay off. What's the worst that can happen? They say no? OK, never mind, they were not the right person for you to network with. Put your big girl (or boy!) pants on and reach out to someone else.

You *literally* have nothing to lose. Even now, after years of running my business, I love it when people reach out to me. I might not actually be able to meet up with every single person but it's nice to get to know people out there.

When you do get together with fellow suppliers make sure you're asking engaging questions. I don't mean that you need to pick their brain, but asking open questions about them, their experiences and their success will all serve up useful information for you. If you're looking for an SEO expert, ask if they have used one. If you're looking for a graphic designer, ask if they can recommend one. Are they members of any great Facebook groups? If so, which ones? Can they add you? Then make sure that if you follow their recommendations you give them a shout out on Instagram. The most important thing is proactivity. Be proactive, be engaging and the rest will be easy.

Get supplier details

Whenever you take a wedding booking it's really important that you ask the couple (in advance) who all of their suppliers are. Put together an easy to complete questionnaire and ask the details of the dress, the florist, the cake maker, the photographer etc. List every single type of supplier. I started to do this after a year or so of running my business and it really was a game changer.

In the run up to the wedding I make sure that I have reached out to every single supplier on that list, even if they are suppliers I wouldn't meet on the day. I make sure that I follow them on social media and also send them a DM there.

I tell them that I'm involved in the same wedding as them and that I'm really excited to be working with them. The response I get always really surprises me. It's often the case that I'm the only supplier that does this, and of course the result is that the suppliers feel really good about building a relationship with me.

On the day of the wedding I always post an Instagram story and make sure I tag all of the suppliers – including those not physically present on the wedding day. Again, it's another touch point with that supplier, each step of the way building respect and trust. The added benefit is also that they will usually share that Instagram story which offers me visibility within their audience – bingo!

After the wedding I follow up with another email to tell them how much I loved their cake/flowers/make-up etc. and that I really hope we will work together again.

Who do you think will be in the forefront of that supplier's mind when they are next asked to recommend a wedding photographer? You bet it'll be me. This simple technique has got me so many bookings over the years, and no matter your position in the industry, I cannot recommend it highly enough.

Blogging

Yes, I can hear all of you sigh. But the thing is, you absolutely must blog. Blogging helps you on a number of levels.

1. Google loves it when you blog. Include all of your keywords and this will help increase Google traffic to your site.

2. You look busy (who do you think a couple will book? The super busy and popular florist or the one who hasn't blogged for three years?). Couples who shop around and come back to your site to see fresh content will be engaged and interested.

3. It gives you the opportunity to credit and compliment all of the suppliers that you already engaged with before the wedding (and hopefully on the wedding day itself). Share the link everywhere you can – if it's on Facebook then tag the other suppliers. Follow up with another direct email and ask them to share your link on their social media channels. It doesn't matter whether you're the photographer or not – if you've gone to the effort to create a blog post the other suppliers will share it. More to the point they will look forward to working with you again because you made it so easy to showcase their work.

Referrals

It's a great idea to have a collection of referrals ready to offer your brides and grooms. Perhaps you might even have a hidden page on your website where you talk about these other fabulous suppliers and name them.

If you're fully booked, it's significantly more within your interest to refer to a 'competitor' than just say you're not available. Why? Because they will almost certainly return the favour.

In that first year of making friends with the photographer I had a major work-crush on, she referred ten bookings to me. That was a total value of £15,000. All because I took the time to say hello.

Create a styled shoot

Styled shoots are one of my favourite ways to network. You're all gathered because you respect each other's work. You want to work together again and you all want to have a great time doing it. One of the most important elements of a styled shoot is to ensure that you collaborate with like-minded suppliers and suppliers who complement your style. Look for people who share a common ideal client, style and brand values. Try at all costs to avoid working on styled shoots that don't have a brief that inspires you and that fits with your brand. I've made that mistake before and it's costly.

So, what do you need to put together a styled shoot? First you need a concept, an idea. I recommend formulating a plan before you start to reach out to other suppliers. Perhaps you could put together a Pinterest board to share your imagination for the project. If needs be perhaps you could create a written piece that tells the story behind the shoot. I've been approached about many styled shoots over the years and I was always vastly more interested in a shoot that had a purpose and had been thought out.

Before you start reaching out to other suppliers. I recommend creating a hit-list of the people you want to be involved. Every styled shoot is different but usually includes: a venue, a model (or models), a dress/suits, flowers, stationery, cake, hair and make-up artist, photographer (and any other details you'd like to include). It's your shoot – you decide.

Once you have created the hit-list of suppliers you'd like involved, it's time to present your plan to them. If you've thought it through properly and targeted people who share common brands, ethos and clients I would expect you to experience some success recruiting a team.

The benefits of a styled shoot are infinite but most importantly it's brilliant fun! Afterwards make sure you utilise your social media sharing and blogging. Don't forget that the team you have worked with now form part of your network. So, check in with those people, be one of their cheerleaders, and where possible recommend them to your clients.

Find your tribe

Finally, here I want to remind you the importance of finding your tribe. The most basic of our human needs is to feel like we belong. Without this we can experience all sorts of unhelpful emotions – emotions that can stand in the way of building a successful business. Finding a tribe of people that will help lift you up, inspire you and motivate you to strive for more will be hugely important to you. Finding the *right* tribe is important though. When I started my coaching business, I was in a few groups and always felt a disconnect. I felt that to be accepted I needed to be more like them and I felt like I had to change who I was. The moment I found the right tribe I realised that being me was my superpower. Surrounded by the right people that's exactly what will happen. Go and find your tribe and love them deeply.

Social Media

Now we are going to take a look at social media and how it can help you build your business. Social media is a tool I definitely recommend you to use and at the time of writing this book I prioritise Instagram, Facebook and Pinterest. There are lots of different platforms available and I encourage you to use the ones that you feel the most synergy with. There is absolutely no need for you to be *everywhere*. If a platform doesn't work for you or you don't enjoy it, it's not right for you and your business. Likewise, it's really important to think about where your clients hang out. If your ideal client isn't someone who is on Instagram, for example, then maybe don't use it.

Before we dive into how you can use these platforms, I first want to talk about the psychology behind using them. Social media can be a hotbed for overwhelm and 'comparisonitis'. It's predominantly image driven and when you're in the early (or in fact any) stage of your business it can feel as though everyone else is creating beautiful imagery and you're not. There will always be someone who is further along in their business, but allowing that to stop you in your tracks will only leave you further behind. My way of coping with the social media overwhelm has always been really simple:

Plan your posts in advance

The least inspired you will ever feel is when you *have* to post but can't think of anything to say. From that energy you will only have one outcome – dashing off a hurried post that doesn't really say anything valuable or important. These posts are a waste of your time and energy. I absolutely recommend planning in advance, as it makes it so much easier. I would diarise a chunk of time each week, or month, and dedicate that time to mapping out my social media. I recommend using a scheduling tool to help with this. There are many available and in most cases are a very small investment that will buy you a lot of time. Later is the app that I currently use, and Planoly is another option.

Switch off notifications

Honestly, I think this was the most liberating thing I ever did. Prior to this I had become like a clicker-trained dog. Every time I heard my phone bing, I picked it up. This is not the way to run a successful and profitable business (or a life that isn't fraught with anxiety, frankly). This would be the shortcut to wasting your time, getting caught up in imposter syndrome and stunting your own creativity.

Be you

I have already talked about how I felt like I needed to become someone else to be accepted. Social media is rife with people carefully curating their lives. Don't compare your real life to someone else's showreel. The best responses I ever get on social media are when I'm showing up, being myself, being raw and honest and open. Be yourself – always.

Know that this is just one piece of the puzzle

Yes, I love social media (most of the time). Yes, I enjoy using it (most of the time). Yes it has brought me enquiries (some of the time) but this is just *one* piece of the puzzle. I see people who are building their wedding business spending ninety-nine per cent of their time on Instagram. This is not going to take you where you want to be. Please don't put all of your eggs in this basket. Remember that you don't own your social media profiles. They could disappear overnight and if it's your only marketing channel this could leave you massively exposed.

Be clear on your strategy

For me, social media serves two purposes. First, I use it for people to learn more about me, how I work, what they can expect of me, and to build the know/like/trust factor. The second purpose is as a channel to direct people to my website. Imagine that your social media is simply like putting a flyer on a notice board. Some people will see it and take action, many people will miss the fact that you are even there. You need that flyer to be captivating enough to entice people to take action and come and visit your shop (i.e. your website).

Instagram

I've always liked Instagram and particularly enjoy using Instagram stories. Many people in the wedding industry enjoy using this platform too. I've put together a top ten tips for using Instagram to build your business.

Use a photo of yourself in your profile picture

I know this sounds really obvious and it's only a teeny tiny picture but it's your first opportunity to go face to face with your clients. People are so much more likely to build a relationship with a human than a logo, so let's see your face.

Have a really clear biography

Your biography is the chunk of text at the top of your profile. I encourage you not to confuse your potential followers/clients by having a wordy biography. Make it crystal clear who you are, what you do and how you can help them. Don't assume that people will know this. Be unique, be creative, be you. If your Instagram handle (i.e. your username, your @) is your business name, your title (the part that shows in bold at the top of your biography) doesn't need to be the same. Use your business keywords here to help you show up in searches. My preference is a bullet pointed biography. This makes it easy and quick to read through and to help make multiple points in what is a limited amount of text.

Post consistently

I hear from wedding suppliers all the time about how they are worried about posting too often and then, as a result, end up not posting at all.

Does that sound like you? I understand that it can be frustrating when you follow someone and they post multiple times a day, but that wouldn't be a strategy I would recommend. If you're keen to use Instagram to grow your business you need to be posting on a consistent basis. That might not be every day for you. I understand that if you're growing your business around your family/your job, time is limited and it might not be possible to post every day. Consistency on Instagram, as with blogging, is way more important. So, decide what timescales work for you and commit to those. I would say that if you're keen to use it to grow your business, a minimum of four times a week is about right. Use the 'insights' to understand what days of the week and what times of the week your followers are mostly using Instagram and test some different outcomes.

Use good quality images

Your followers do not want to see poor quality or blurry images. You are guaranteed to lose them this way. If you're not a photographer or someone who enjoys taking pictures, I would strongly recommend that you either practise taking good phone photos or build a relationship with a photographer. The phones we have nowadays have exceptionally good cameras. It is possible to take some great pictures and edit them to look professional. Professional photos will always look best though, so please make sure you follow my guidance in the networking module to build relationships with photographers. As one myself I can tell you I am incredibly happy to share my images with suppliers who credit my work.

Get personal

I've already talked about being yourself, but please don't forget the importance of actually showing your face. So many suppliers are hiding behind their brands and this makes it virtually impossible for us to build up an idea of who you are and how well we will work together. Your people want to see you! I recommend at least one in every nine posts should be of you. Tell us about yourself and your story. People who are going to pay you money desperately want to hear that.

Engage with your ideal client

It sounds obvious but this is a very important point to share. When I talked about understanding your ideal client, I covered this off, but to remind you – you don't need to be the person on Instagram trying to please everyone.

Build a loyal following of *ideal clients* by being you and speaking only to them. Really feel how you can educate and serve your perfect audience. How are you solving their problem? If you don't yet have enough images that showcase your best work, go and create them.

Ask questions

Sometimes nobody will answer you and that is OK. I've heard the sweet sound of tumbleweed on many occasions and honestly, I will never lose any sleep over it. Because *sometimes* it'll blow up into a huge discussion and you'll find yourself having created 'viral' content. Very early on I tried this and edited one wedding photo two ways – one in colour, and one in black and white. I posted it with a very simple caption "Black and white or colour?" Wow, I had over 300 comments (prior to this I was lucky to have more than one) and got a booking off the back of it – think outside the box.

Use Instagram stories

I love Instagram stories. I know from personal experience how easy it is to get caught up in having the 'perfect' grid, and stories allow us to be just that little bit more unedited. I find them particularly useful for showing the behind-the-scenes stuff that just isn't as relevant for grid posts. I believe they also work really well from a human instinct perspective. We grow up to automatically read top to bottom, left to right. When you open Instagram, the first thing you see in the top left is a story, so our instinct is to click on it. Be that person who is regularly there and waiting to be watched by your followers. Remember to tag people so that other accounts share your story.

Go live

I know what you're thinking and I felt that way too. It's along the lines of 'absolutely no way', right? Stick with me, I promise you this is a great way to grow your business. In the Instagram stories reel, live broadcasts take priority over regular stories and will be the very first thing people see at the top left of their feed. Social media is very quickly responding to people's desire to consume video content. The future is film, so jump in now and see how it could work for you. The added benefit of lives is that your followers are also notified when you go live. This does wonders for your visibility.

Use a hashtag strategy

The goalposts change on this all the time, and I could honestly write a whole book on this alone. In fact, in The Wedding Business Club I have a course that takes people a month to complete. The subject is huge. So let's keep it clear and simple. With every post that you make on Instagram you have the opportunity to use thirty hashtags. Hashtags are keywords or phrases that use no spaces and have the # at the beginning. In Instagram, you can search for content that includes particular hashtags and you can follow hashtags, just as you would follow an account. So why is this important? Well, think of a couple planning their wedding. Perhaps your ideal client might search something like #bohoweddingideas. Your aim should be to show up in the searches for hashtags that your ideal client is using. Think about what they might be searching for and make sure you are using those hashtags in your posts.

I hope these points start to build an idea for you of how best to use Instagram. Most importantly I invite you to be *yourself*. People buy from people, and in particular they buy from people they know, like and trust. So, think about how you can show up in this way.

Facebook

Facebook seems to have taken a dip in popularity with lots of wedding suppliers preferring Instagram, but Facebook is still a very important piece of my marketing puzzle. Of course, it works in a different way, but there are some amazing things that you can do on Facebook that you can't on Instagram. I want to kick off by reminding you some of the easy things you can do to pimp your Facebook page for free.

Brand your page

Facebook gives you a lot of page space to communicate your brand, so make sure you are using it. Regularly change your profile picture (using a photo of you, please) and your cover picture. I find using the cover photo to publish offers works well for me. I recommend using canva. com to create some graphics that include your brand, a photo of you and some text around your offering.

Use announcements/pinned posts

I love that on Facebook you can pin (or mark as an announcement) a post that you'd like people to see first when they visit your page. I recommend that you pin your very best blog post to the top of your page. This does a few things for your potential clients. It immediately shows them you're brilliant and right for them and it guides them away from your 'flyer' (social media) into your shop (your website!).

Link your Facebook page to Instagram

As Facebook owns both platforms, linking them is super simple. I recommend setting up your Instagram account to always automatically post to Facebook. You can do this quickly and easily by heading into your settings in Instagram. This means that you're not forgetting about your Facebook page and it's getting regular fresh content.

Share blog posts

One of the amazing features of Facebook is that you can share your blog post links. This is a big opportunity because you can literally walk people away from social media into your shop (remember, that's your website). Every time you blog, I recommend that you share it on your Facebook page. Don't forget to tag all of the suppliers mentioned in the blog post and follow up with a direct message asking them to share on their pages, too. And don't be afraid to share older blog posts if they are still posts that you love.

Go live

Facebook lives usually result in a higher exposure for me than Instagram (even though my Instagram following is higher) so if I really want to step up my visibility and my exposure, going live on Facebook works really well. If you've never gone live before, I know that it will feel scary. Trust me I was terrified the first time I did it, but the result totally outweighs the fear. As soon as you start to experience results (i.e. bookings) you'll forget that you were ever scared.

Use your personal profile

It states in Facebook user terms that you should never use a personal Facebook profile for commercial gain. Indeed, I know people who have had their profiles suspended for this. So of course, you need to think carefully about how you do this. But certainly, sharing content from your Facebook business page onto your personal profile is totally acceptable and means that people you are friends with can be exposed to your content. I also recommend using your personal profile cover photo as an opportunity to tell people who you are and what you do. Creating a quick and simple graphic using canva.com makes this really easy and helps people understand what you do. Never take for granted the fact that your Facebook friends can and will want to help and support you to grow your business.

I hope this gives you an idea of how you can use Facebook. I love the fact that you can direct traffic from Facebook to your website, so ensure that you are facilitating this for your potential clients.

Pinterest

We're now going to take a closer look at Pinterest. Even though it sits within the social media bracket, it is really more akin to a search engine. Pinterest is a wonderful, priceless resource for anyone planning a wedding (and indeed anything else). It's a place to find inspiration and generate ideas. Again, this is a huge subject area and could really warrant a book of its own, but for now I want to help you get started.

So, as with Instagram and Facebook, my sole intention is to take people away from Pinterest and to my website. I have no other motive for using Pinterest than this. The best way to do this is to post beautiful, inspirational and on-brand content for your ideal clients, which includes a backlink to take people to your website.

When you are posting on Pinterest these images absolutely *must* include a backlink your website. If you are unable to physically pin from your website you can copy and paste the URL into an uploaded image (but of course this takes time and makes the process laborious). Pinterest makes this super easy for you by having a browser extension button (if the idea of that feels overwhelming, Pinterest make it *very* easy – google it and you'll find the Pinterest instructions). This means that whenever you hover over your pictures on your website, a pin will appear and all you have to do is click it to start the process of pinning to one of your boards.

I also recommend that you head to your Pinterest settings and 'claim' your website. This simply means formalising the relationship between your Pinterest account and your website. By doing this, some of the information you include on your website images will automatically be included on your pins. This includes copying and pasting a tiny bit of code into the header of your website. Pinterest are really good at explaining this, but if you're struggling you can always ask your website designer to do this for you.

In my Pinterest account I use a series of inspirational boards to motivate and serve my prospective website visitors. These include venue specific boards for my favourite venues and ideas boards for make-up, hair, dresses, cakes and many other things. I want people to feel like they've *arrived* when they find my boards and really immerse themselves in the imagery. Of course, ultimately, I want them to then come to my website.

I recommend upgrading your personal account to a business account if you haven't already done so. It's free and easy to do and allows you to use their analytics information. This is really useful to understand exactly how much traffic you are sending to your website.

One of the questions I am asked most about Pinterest is whether I recommend 'pinning' other people's content. Usually I recommend the eighty-twenty rule. Eighty per cent of your pins should be your pictures from your website and the other twenty per cent should be other people's pins. I know it seems counterintuitive to do this but it helps with your visibility and your relationships with other accounts.

It's easy to assume that Pinterest is all about images but actually my experience shows that using words on images works really well. Pinterest has the ability to read the words on your pins and my experience shows that people enjoy the contrast between images and text. Think about some graphics that you could put together on Canva that offer useful information to your potential clients. You can post those on your blog and then pin those straight onto your Pinterest boards.

Think carefully about what you are naming your images. If you're anything like me I typically export my images with a title like 'James & Sarah' (i.e. my couples' names). This isn't a compelling enough title to show up in searches on Pinterest. Try to name your images using the keywords you want to be found by, or the venue or other suppliers you would like to be found for.

Make Pinterest part of your workflow. I will talk more about workflow in the Business section, but in essence, I want you to think about how you can pin pictures of every single client you ever work with that fits your ideal-client profile. Part of this will be to create a blog post for each couple and pin all of the pictures from that blog post. You can use a scheduling tool, like Tailwind for example, to help ensure a consistent pinning process. As with all social media and blogging, consistency is vitally important and will help you build a bigger audience.

Out of all of the social media I use, Pinterest takes the least amount of time and rewards me with the most website hits. Yep, you heard that right. Prioritising Pinterest will be a wonderful use of your time and I strongly recommend that you get stuck into this amazing platform.

The most important message I can leave you with when it comes to social media is that this really is just one piece of the whole puzzle. If you're spending hours and hours on this and not reaping the rewards, now is the time to change. Social media can be, and should be, a fabulous tool but you must balance its use with all of the other plates that you need to keep spinning.

Marketing Summary

Before moving onto the next section of this book I want you to ensure that you:

- Have understood the importance of writing captivating copy and know how you are going to create this for your business.

- Have started to map out a networking strategy that will help increase the visibility of you and your business.

- Understand how social media can be a wonderful platform for your business and have started to carve out content to increase your visibility.

Book Bonuses

I've created a library of resources that are yours for free. Come over to www.fayecornhillcoaching.co.uk/bookbonuses where you'll find a library of premade social media graphics, which are yours to use for free.

Part Four

Business

In this section we are going to be looking at exactly how you configure the nuts and bolts of your business so that it runs smoothly and seamlessly. The processes and systems you use can significantly change how easy your business is to run.

Selling

In this chapter we are going to take a deep dive into exactly how you can sell your service or your product to your ideal client. I know that most people wince at the idea of selling and I do understand how you feel. I consider myself lucky because selling has always been a passion of mine. Remember that seven-year-old Faye was always working on a business idea and, even though it broke all the school rules, I knew how to get people to hand over their money. It felt natural for me.

After graduating I went on to spend more than ten years in corporate sales, and during that time I carved out a method that worked for me, without fail. That very method has helped me sell technology, recruitment, logistics, services and of course wedding photography. It's also a method I have taught hundreds of wedding suppliers and time and time again I get the same feedback – it works.

Before we get into the nuts and bolts of the method, I want to talk to you about selling and why it doesn't have to feel awkward and icky.

What is selling?

Very simply, selling is the art of persuasion. It's an exchange between two parties. Sounds simple, doesn't it? Your business success is intrinsically linked to your ability to sell, which is why the concept is so important and also the reason that so many people avoid it.

Simply put, without selling you won't make any money, and I know you're here to make money – am I right? I strongly believe that if you are not 'selling' to potential clients, they could struggle to feel excited about your service or your product. We assume that people don't want to be 'sold to' but I believe this couldn't be further from the truth. People who are interested in your proposition want to hear about you, your story, your service and your product. For a paying client, the lack of being 'sold to' can often result in them not fully understanding how much you would like to have them as a client. I truly believe that, when done in the right way, people *appreciate* being sold to.

Let me bring in an example here, because recently I bought a new car. On the first day of buying my new car I went into two showrooms and experienced wildly different service.

In the first showroom, it took a while for a salesperson to approach me and when he did he was friendly, relaxed and offered me a brochure. He said to let him know if I had any questions and he also told me that the model I was looking at had a fancy stereo system and newly upgraded large wheels.

My observations were:

- He didn't ask me *any* questions therefore he had no idea what my buying criteria was.

- As he didn't understand what my buying criteria was, he was unable to position any of the features that would have been of interest to me.

- As he wasn't able to position any of the features that I was interested in, I found it hard to feel any sort of excitement about this particular car.

- He let me walk out of the door without taking my contact details. As such I didn't feel valued at all by this person.

In the second showroom I was immediately greeted by a sales person who asked whether I would like him to answer any of my questions or whether I'd just like to have a look around. When I told him I'd just like to have a quick look he agreed and said he'd pop back in a bit to see what I thought. After adequate time of looking around he came back and actively asked what interested me most about this car. He asked what questions I had and how I would most like to proceed.

My observations were these:

- I felt immediate rapport with this person – he showed the right level of interest in me but it didn't feel over the top. He picked up on my excitement for buying a new car and mirrored this back. He gave me the choice of how I would like to experience the viewing which made me feel valued and made it seem like the service was bespoke.

- He immediately understood my buying criteria, which was nothing to do with fancy sound systems or big wheels. As he asked the right questions, he quickly understood that I wanted a reliable and safe electric car that had space enough for my children and dog.

- As a result of understanding my buying criteria, he was able to propose the features of the car he knew were important to me. We didn't once talk about the internal gadgetry.

- When I left the showroom, he asked how I would like to proceed. He asked politely and courteously whether he could follow up with an email. I didn't think twice about saying yes. This man was offering a completely personal service and I felt incredibly valued as a customer. I wanted him to take my details, I wanted him to call me because I wanted to buy this car and I wanted to buy it from him.

It's not rocket science to work out who got my business. I bought the car from that second showroom.

There are many myths about selling including:

> People won't book me if I sell because it seems pushy.
> People don't want to be sold to.
> I don't need to sell if people like me.
> Selling puts people off.
> People always buy based on price.

There is only one way to sell.
You have to do whatever it takes to get the sale.
Buyers don't spend over their budget.

Not one of these is true. The truth is that when it comes to selling, we have built up ideas and preconceptions about what people think about us, and our ego is stopping us from the potential embarrassment of judgement.

I want you to think right now about what is stopping you from selling to your potential clients. It's probably one of these:

You're worried what people will say.
You don't understand your product.
You don't feel confident in your service or product.
You lack belief in your own abilities.
You're scared of someone saying no.
You don't know how to sell.
You're afraid people won't like you.
You're afraid your image will be ruined if you sell.
You're too good to be a sales person.
You're professional and selling is bad.
You have more important things to do.

The great news is that I am going to show you exactly how to use my Easy Selling Method. When you understand how to use this, all of these judgements will go and you'll wish you'd found it before. So, let's dive right in.

The Easy Selling Method

The Easy Selling Method is broken down into six stages. This method can be used from the moment you receive an email enquiry and it's the exact system I use to this day.

1. Research

The first stage of the method is research. As soon as an email enquiry lands in my inbox, I spend ample time looking into it. On my enquiry form I ask which venue the couple are getting married at, so I spend time researching this. Have I worked there before (and therefore do I have photo examples I could send in my follow up)? Is it actually a venue I *want* to work at again (and therefore can I facilitate this enquiry)? I then head straight over to social media and I look for the person who has sent the enquiry. On my enquiry form I ask for the bride and the groom's full names for this very purpose. Sometimes you won't be able to find people but it is most certainly worth a go. If I can find them, I ask myself whether they look like the sort of couple who would be a good fit for me. Sometimes that is virtually impossible to tell but I recommend looking for clues that help you build rapport.

Example

I had an enquiry once from a bride. I found her on Facebook and her profile picture was of her walking a black Labrador. This is always a bingo moment for me because I have a black lab. Black lab owners are magnetised to each other. I cannot tell you how many weddings I have done that involved black labs – it's like a super niche I never knew I could have! When I eventually spoke to this client, I weaved this theme into our conversation which is an instant rapport booster. Always look for the clues!

2. Ask

The first client approach, whether via an email reply, a call or a face-to-face meeting should always be your opportunity to ask questions. It's absolutely imperative that you are being interactive and interested in them, their lives and of course their wedding.

I have tested my hit rate on email responses when I do/don't ask questions. I found that potential clients are fifty per cent more likely to reply when I finish my email on a question. It's human nature to want to respond to a question. Plus, someone planning a wedding feels like they are the only person to have ever done so. They *want* to talk to you; they *want* to tell you all about their plans. So be interested, and ask questions.

Top tip: Always go into a phone consultation or a face-to-face meeting with a list of questions. It means that you won't forget to ask the key questions and also shows that you're organised, professional and interested. Here are some examples of powerful questions you could try:

- What is most important to you about your wedding photography?
- Who else is involved in the decision making for your wedding flowers?
- When are you hoping to make a decision by?
- How will you know when you have met the right make-up artist?
- How important for you is it that you have a really good relationship with your wedding planner?

Top tip: Think about what you want to sell them, and try to get them to tell you they need this right at the beginning of the conversation.

3. Listen

When you're keen to sell to a potential client it's easy to fall into the trap of sell, sell, sell – even if you consciously don't *want* to. Demonstrate to your potential client that you are actively listening, it goes a long way in building rapport and trust. Be genuinely interested in what they have to say. Remove all distractions and take notes. Don't just sit there waiting to talk, let what they have told you sink in before you jump back in with an answer.

Top tip: Listen out for your clients' values. Everyone buys based on values and the best way to bond with a client is to find this common ground.

4. Teach

So, by this stage you know exactly what your client wants. You have asked fabulous questions, listened intently to the answers and made notes. This is your opportunity to tell the potential client exactly how you can help them. Tell them all about the features of your service or product that they have told you they are looking for. Tell them about you, your story and why you do what you do. Tell them why you are the best choice. This gets easier with practice, and I would spend some time working on a little paragraph you can use at this point. Think back to the target client paragraph you created when we covered off ideal clients and build on that. Having a pre-prepared 'pitch' will really help you out if you're worried you might forget what to say. Rehearse it so that it comes naturally to you.

Top tip: Focus on what they told you was important to them and sell it right back to them.

5. Qualify

This is so often the piece of the puzzle that is missing and could well be the reason you're not converting enquiries. To qualify your potential client, you need to overcome their objections, you need to answer all of their outstanding questions and you need to clear any doubt that is still in their mind. And you do this by asking one simple question, something like:

> "Are you still feeling nervous about xyz?" (the thing they told you they were nervous about during the Ask phase).
> "Have you got any reservations about me or my service?"
> "What questions haven't I answered that would enable you to book me?"
> "Does anything I've said sound like it's not right for you?"

If at this stage they bring things up, you can go back to the Teach stage and talk them through that particular part of your proposition. When you've done this, you can qualify again until they are totally happy. You might have to go back to the Teach stage twice, three times, maybe more. And that's OK – your client needs more information. A request for more information is absolutely a buying signal. If they weren't interested, they wouldn't ask.

6. Close

If you've asked enough questions and listened actively to their buying criteria. If you've positioned your product/service according to what they've told you they need and you have overcome their objections through the qualification, this bit should be easy!

Don't be afraid of asking for the business. If you're currently at this stage saying 'OK, have a think and let me know' then please, STOP. It might sound friendly but it's not getting you the sale. When closing you should be asking questions that forces the potential client to say YES or NO. Examples could be:

> "Are you ready to book?"
> "Would you like me to tell you my booking procedure?"
> "Shall I email you my contract?"
> "Would you like me to book your wedding date in my diary?"

When you've asked your closing question it's incredibly important that you then let the client speak. The tendency is to fill the silence with justification or chit-chat. No, this is the stage where you wait, however long it takes, for the client to give you a YES or NO. Of course, there will be times that you can't close in the same way. For example, if you're only speaking to the bride but she needs to speak to her fiancé. This is absolutely fine but the close should still be there, it just needs to be tweaked. For example, "Would Wednesday at 2pm be a good time for me to call again to discuss our conversation with your fiancé?" Then, silence. The close is simply a verbal agreement to further your relationship. So, while they might not be saying yes to signing the contract, find a way to further the relationship with them saying yes to you.

This is the Easy Selling Method and I genuinely hope you're excited about taking it out into the world and trying it out. It's an amazing strategy that I know will help you get clients over the line.

Pricing

How do I price my wedding business? It's the question I am asked about almost every day. And genuinely there isn't a one size fits all approach. The services and products that you offer your clients vary greatly and your pricing model needs to be bespoke to you.

For the purpose of helping you decide which direction is best for you, I am going to walk you through the model that I use with my clients, which should absolutely shed some light on creating your own pricing strategy. As with many parts of your business, pricing should evolve. To put this into perspective, I've sold wedding photography packages that are ten times higher than the original price I charged. No, it didn't happen overnight and yes, I invested in myself and my business to be able to do this.

Before we dive into even thinking about how much you should charge, we need to talk about mindset. I know we've had a whole section of the book focus on mindset already but my experience shows that it's during the pricing stage of your business that the mind monkeys tend to spring up. Developing a mindset that will support a confident attitude towards pricing will help you so much.

I want to be absolutely clear. I still experience moments of worry and doubt about my pricing. Typically, after a price increase, when I perhaps haven't received an enquiry for a little while, my mind can flicker towards the negative. And that's OK. It's normal to feel this way. The mindset work I have done doesn't ever stop me from having these thoughts, it simply empowers me to not jump head first into making knee-jerk reactions. I've spoken to so many wedding suppliers who dug deep and found the courage to raise their prices, only to panic and drop them a week later. This feeds your fixed mindset into believing that you're not worthy or good enough and it's not a mindset I want for you.

So, with that in mind, first off, we need to talk about the concept of a fixed mindset and a growth mindset. Someone with a fixed mindset towards pricing will avoid price increases. They will think "nobody will ever pay those sorts of prices" and will ignore everyone around them telling them to raise their rates. Someone with a fixed mindset will look at other suppliers and think "How can s/he *get away* with charging those sorts of prices?" They might watch newer suppliers come into the industry and feel irritated by someone with less experience charging more.

Does this sound like you? If so, I don't want you to panic or to feel judged, I just want you to be honest with yourself. I'll hold my hands up and tell you that this is exactly how I used to feel. I remember so clearly exhibiting at a local wedding show once and finding it completely outrageous that a 'newer' photographer than me was there and was charging more than I was. At the time I couldn't believe the nerve of it. *Who was she, with less experience than me, coming into 'my' patch and charging more.* "Who does she think she is?"

It makes me feel disappointed that I felt this way, it wasted a lot of my time and I don't want this for you. Clearly at that time I didn't fully understand the importance of mindset and I certainly didn't anticipate the knock-on effect it was having on my business.

The opposite mindset to this is a growth mindset. A wedding supplier with a growth mindset is someone who constantly looks for ways to improve and perfect their craft, and, in the long term, to be in a position to raise their rates. This person sees price increases as a challenge and learns from rejection. This person watches other people putting their prices up and finds it motivating rather than threatening. This is absolutely the mindset I have now, but is not one that I developed overnight.

There were many things I did (and still do) to help with my money mindset which, as you know, include journalling, meditation, reading, asking for help, mixing with positive people with growth mindsets and agreeing with myself to cease the negative mind chatter.

We talked about this when we discussed your money mindset, but a quick reminder for you – not everyone is or needs to be your client. You don't *need* everyone to book you. There are nearly eight billion people in this world, you need less than 0.000001 per cent of the world to be your clients. You don't need to exercise a scarcity mindset to attract this number of people, there are plenty of clients just waiting to book you, there are plenty to go around.

So, moving this concept onto how you actually price your product and service is the next stage to really developing your growth mindset. I know from personal experience that you are doing your clients a disservice if you charge too little. Your energy won't be fully in it, your client won't be getting the best version of you, their result won't be the best outcome. Maybe just reading this will trigger some people, and that's OK. I know that some of you might be thinking that I'm wrong and that you would always show up and give 100 per cent, no matter what the payment. This is a lovely idea, but it's one I disagree with.

When you charge a price that feels truly exciting, everything changes. Your energy, your commitment, your attention and your vibration will be different. You will play 'big'. Naturally by playing big and by showing up with this different level of energy, your eyes will be just that little bit wider open. You will see things you couldn't before, you will be tuned into the most inspired and creative version of yourself. You will consistently look for ways to create work that is bigger, better and more inspirational. This very moment is the turning point that you can and will experience if you choose to. Please remember that pricing is not really about the numbers, it's about how you feel in your heart.

How to price your business

So, you're wondering how to get to grips with the nuts and bolts of actually figuring out what to charge? Now I'm going to introduce you to my reverse engineering model of pricing your business. There are, of course, exceptions to this pricing model so bear with me. If this doesn't work for your business model, I'll be coming to you shortly.

First off, I want you to start at the end.

1. Decide on your annual income goal

What's your financial goal? If you've done the work in the goal setting chapter then you will know this already, and if not please head back and do that work. This number should be how much money you take from your business.

2. Decide on the annual cost of running your business

Then I want you to start with your bottom line. Think about all the expenses you incur when you run your business. If you have been running your business for a while, go back through your old accounts and figure this out. Think of every single aspect it costs to run your business including travel, parking, petrol, gifts, food, packaging, postage, supplies, internet, subscriptions etc. etc. If you're new to running your business then it's going to be an educated guess for you. Most things you can work out, for others you might need to estimate for now until you know the reality.

3. Decide how many clients you can work with per year

Next, I want you to work out how much time you have and therefore how many clients it is realistic for you to work with each year. This may be where a lot of people slip up or overestimate how many clients it is sensible for them to work with. Work out exactly the implication of working with each client and how feasible that is for your life and your family.

The final stage is to work out your average price per client. You can do this by adding together your income goal and your expenses, then dividing this by the number of clients you are able to work with.

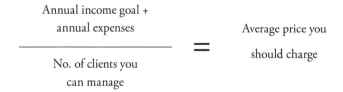

So, let's take an example here. Let's take an annual income goal of £20k with annual expenses that equal £5k. You have the time to work with twenty clients per year so therefore our sum would look like this:

$$\frac{£20k + £5k}{20} = £1,250 \text{ per client}$$

Now you might do this sum and have a eureka moment. If that's the case then brilliant! You might also do the sum and have a horrible sinking feeling that something doesn't add up. Also, OK and not proof that the sum didn't work, but rather evidence that we need to look closer at some of the numbers.

It might be that in reality, to make the sort of money you want to make you need more time. This was a situation I experienced when I was working full time. I knew that I wanted to make more money, but I didn't have enough time to service all of those clients. That was the turning point for me, when I realised that to truly be able to spread my wings and make the money I wanted to, I had to leave my job. It was too easy to pile the pressure onto myself to achieve a certain turnover but if I couldn't physically serve that number of clients, and so it was never going to happen for me.

There are many variables in this calculation and it's one that will be different for everyone. Look closely at the moving pieces:

- your annual income target,
- your expenses, and
- the number of clients you can facilitate.

All of these numbers can be manipulated to get the picture to a place you are happy. Maybe you need to work with more clients (therefore you need more time). Or maybe you need to work with fewer clients (therefore you need to raise your rates to make the same turnover). Play around with the numbers until you find an equation that feels right for you.

The most important part is remaining open-minded with these numbers and work with them until you are happy with the picture you have painted for your business. And remember that this is just a starting point. From here you can start to build out packages and/or collections that serve your clients.

Of course, there are always exceptions to the rules. Typically, florists, stationery designers and cake makers have a more difficult time when it comes to working out the costs of running their business. This is because usually there is some element of wastage and they are required to order more supplies than is strictly necessary to cover for mistakes and/or damaged goods. The method of pricing remains the same though, always work out your income target and your costs first during the quoting stage and ensure you add a percentage on to your raw costs for wastage.

You might have noticed that I haven't yet talked about looking at what anyone else is charging, and there's a good reason for that. I want you to get familiar with your numbers first, *before* you plough into what other people are charging. You don't have the same aspirations and/or costs as your competitors so simply copying and pasting what they do will not fulfil *your* goals.

Having said that, market research is a very important part of pricing your business and something I absolutely encourage you to do. What I'm not doing is talking about lighting the flame of comparisonitis. But I do recommend sense checking your pricing against three other suppliers with whom you consider to be in the same market as yourself. Ideally, these would be people who you identified during the networking chapter as a potential for referral. Take some time to look through their websites and pricing and see how you compare. Again, what you are charging will be different – they are not working towards your goals and aspirations. But it will offer a useful sense check for what is out there in the market for your potential clients.

Systems

For the creatives among us, the idea of 'systems' can feel a bit clunky and perhaps a little dull, but the truth is that a business is only as good as its systems. My corporate days mean I know very well that the best time to implement a system is before I need it. When I started my business, I was fresh faced and selective over the advice I took, including my own. It seemed counterintuitive spending time setting up a 'booking' system when I had no bookings or a 'workflow' system when I didn't actually have any work. But of course, when the bookings and work came and I was suddenly being swallowed up, it was then a far worse time to start creating effective systems.

For some of you, this might feel like a slightly boring topic and I encourage you with all my heart to shift this mindset. Good systems will save your bacon and they will keep you sane. I love spreadsheets. Not because I actually *love* spreadsheets, but I love the feeling they give me – control, organisation and peace of mind. These are priceless in the height of a busy wedding season.

So, now we are going to specifically look at systems that I encourage you to put in place. In fact, I don't encourage, I insist.

Email

I'm pretty sure that most readers of this book have an email system set up but if you don't, you need one ASAP. There are many good email providers out there but my personal choice is Gmail. There are many reasons I use Gmail but here are a few of them:

1. I can use my business email address which forwards into my Gmail inbox. If you haven't yet set up a business email address, I strongly recommend that you do so. It's quick, simple and cheap and sets you apart from people using businessname@gmail.com type email addresses. I set my email addresses up with my website hosting company and they were free, plus the company actually set up a forward so that they come into my Gmail inbox. This works particularly well if you have multiple email addresses that you manage.

2. Gmail makes it very easy to set up an attractive signature which is branded and includes CTAs. This helps you offer your clients a fully branded experience when they deal with you.

3. Template responses are a hugely important part of my business model and Gmail allows me to create a range of these to quickly and easily insert into my email responses. So, for instance, when I receive an enquiry, it takes me around fifteen seconds to reply with a well written and thorough response that I can quickly edit to make bespoke.

Calendar

An online calendar is an absolute must for any business owner. I do love a paper diary and still carry around my trusty notepad which details my movements for the week. But behind the scenes I couldn't survive without my online calendar. The reality is that a paper diary can be lost, an online calendar cannot. If your paper diary is your only source of client records, you really do need to change this ASAP. Double booking or losing contact details is no joke in this industry.

I use Google Calendar which links quickly and easily to my email. I can quickly add appointments, tasks and link emails to calendar entries. Most importantly I can also link my Google Calendar to my husband's calendar. This is absolutely imperative for me, as a mother of two children who have a vastly more buoyant social life than I do. Yes, it can be a juggle but having an up-to-date online calendar makes booking appointments with clients quick and easy and avoids me having to go back to rearrange with clients because I forgot I was doing the ballet class pickup.

Accounting

My accounting system caused me a lot of frustration for a long time. I tried so hard to avoid ever outsourcing this because I was just seeing the cost and never looking at the benefit of working with a professional. Let me tell you, a good accountant will save you money, not cost you money. The first year I worked with an accountant I estimated that they saved me £500 and, more importantly, took away all of the stress and bother that I had previously been incurring. Company accounting is a serious matter and should be completed accurately and on time. My accountant helps me feel confident and secure about my accounting responsibilities and she helps me take advantage of claiming for everything I possibly can.

Aside from this, my accountant introduced me to working with a proper accounting software which made bookkeeping so much easier. There are many software systems out there – Xero, QuickBooks and Sage to name a few. Most of them offer a fourteen-day free trial period so I recommend trying them out and seeing what works well for you. Most of them also have apps that will allow you to record receipts while you are on the go. They also allow you to quickly and efficiently invoice your clients and some also let clients pay online using a credit card.

As your business grows, the accounting responsibilities grow too. Having a relationship with an accountant who can help navigate you through that period will be invaluable. The benefit of an accountant, and accounting software, hugely outweighs the cost and I highly recommend that you go and find one that works well for you.

Workflow

The main purpose of a workflow is to keep you organised and sane. Before having a workflow, I would find myself getting completely overwhelmed by what I had/hadn't completed for each client. As a result, my clients were experiencing varying levels of service from me. Some would get all the bells and whistles and some would just get the bells. Not a service level I was proud of.

A workflow doesn't need to be elaborate or complicated. Early on for me, it was a simple spreadsheet that detailed each of the tasks I needed to complete for each client. This included the timescales for each task and from this spreadsheet I would make diary entries as reminders.

Nowadays there are some companies that offer workflow software that does the leg work for you. Systems like 17Hats, Trello, Asana, Lightblue (for photographers) or Studio Ninja (also for photographers) can be a godsend during a busy wedding season. Again, most of these offer free trial periods so I recommend you go and see which ones work best for you. Some of these also incorporate invoicing and accounting too.

Contracts

A contract is not a 'nice to have', it is a must. If you are currently exchanging money for your product and/or service and you are not protecting yourself and your client with a contract, you need to address this now. I'm not a qualified lawyer so I'm not here to offer you legal advice but I am a Business Coach who can tell you from personal experience that you will one day rely on your contract to protect you. If you don't have one you are completely exposed.

My advice to you is to seek legal support from a legally trained professional to help you write your contract. It might seem like just another thing you need to do but in actual fact this 'piece of paper' could potentially save your business one day. It needs to be watertight. Some lawyers have really good contract templates that you can use which can be a cost-effective way of protecting yourself. Make sure that you are engaging with a professional and someone who specialises in the law in the country where you are based and where you operate. If you work with weddings overseas, you may well need to consult a lawyer from that country to fully understand the legal practice of that country.

I recommend using an online signature software to process contracts. Printing them off and scanning or posting them back to you just holds up the process and allows people time to delay, dawdle or indeed change their minds. I know this isn't the most sexy subject (unless you're a spreadsheet geek like me!) but I really do encourage you to get yourself organised and ready for success.

Business Summary

In this section of the book I want you to have:

- Understood the importance of selling yourself and your product/service.

- Understood The Easy Selling Method so that you are ready to use it when your next enquiry comes in.

- Considered your pricing model and re-worked this if the method I used has highlighted gaps in your current strategy.

- Started to map out some new systems that will help you to run your business smoothly.

Book Bonuses

I've created a library of resources that are yours for free. Come over to www.fayecornhillcoaching.co.uk/bookbonuses where you'll find:

1. The Easy Selling Method cheat sheet
2. Cashflow spreadsheet
3. Workflow spreadsheet

A Final Word

Well, my friends, the time has come for me to wish you on your way and send you into the wonderful world of weddings. I hope with all my heart that this book has been a useful resource for you. It was never on my agenda to write a book. In fact, when the idea was first presented to me, I laughed awkwardly and said that I didn't really have much to say. Turns out that wasn't true. The wedding industry is a sacred place to me. It's enabled me to dream in a bigger way than I'd ever dreamt before, it's allowed me the space to feel truly creative and ultimately it has enabled me to live the life I chose.

Many people ask me about the best advice I would give anyone starting in the industry. Obviously, I will now tell them to read this book because I have put *everything* in here. I'd like to think of it as the go-to for wedding business owners, but of course, I'm still learning and will continue to learn every day. So, what I'd say is that life is jam-packed with lessons. Sometimes you will feel on top of the world and in your creative and business zone of genius, and on other days you will feel like a complete failure and wonder what on earth you were even thinking of when you started your business.

When that happens, I want you to come back, pick up this book and head straight for the mindset chapter. I believe so passionately in the power of your mindset and want that always to be your number one focus.

Be patient in your pursuit. Be kind to yourself and know that sometimes you might take a wrong turn, because life won't always go your way. I want to remind you that you always have the choice in how you react. In life and in business it is my firm belief that you either win or learn. So, when the chips are down the best thing you can do is look for the learning. It is always there, no matter how much you try to cover it up. High achieving people (who usually operate a growth mindset!) don't wallow in the losing zone. They look at a situation, analyse what happened, look for the lesson and find a way forward. Be that person in the wedding industry and you will naturally catapult yourself forward.

I'm not special. I just did the basics well and consistently. When people around me 'couldn't be bothered' or blamed something or someone else for the lack of their success, I hung in there. I kept going, I looked for new and different ways to achieve. I made myself a commitment very early on to give myself the best possible chance of success. I couldn't do that without going all in and consistently showing up for myself. Be that version of you.

If you're at a stage in your life and business where you need to make some decisions, I implore you not to shy away from them. Your life will have the series of T-junction moments that will define your future. It's not chance or coincidence or luck – you choose. I've had to make some crazy decisions in my life as a business owner. Things that make me feel uncomfortable just thinking about right now. It takes courage to follow your heart in business because there is so much which is unknown. Maybe you've got no experience, maybe you're the first in your family to start a business, maybe you've got the desire to leave a successful career and start over – whatever it is, trust that you are feeling this for a reason. Listen to your intuition and your heart and let them be the navigation tools for your future, and not what other people say, and not what other people do.

Don't wait for tomorrow or next year, don't wait for experience, for money, for love or for a skinny bum. Take a chance on yourself now. I believe in you. I'm addicted to being courageous. I know it sounds mad but I love the buzz of taking the brave route. I get nervous, of course I do, but I love the feeling of those incredible emotions that come with it: excitement, nerves, pride, trepidation and joy. Get addicted to courage and you'll experience new heights. I say this completely detaching myself from the outcome. Sometimes it doesn't work out for me but if I have shown up with all my courageous guns blazing, I'm winning and absolutely nobody can stop me.

There are many tools that make up the toolkit of a wedding business owner but the greatest tool you have is *yourself*. You are the reason you will be successful. Embrace yourself, love yourself and *be* yourself always.

Are you ready for the next chapter? Good, because for that chapter YOU are the author. Grab a pen and paper and start now. There is no time like the present.

Love, Faye x

What's Next?

Connect with the Author

📷 @fayecornhill

f facebook.com/FayeCornhillCoaching

🌐 www.fayecornhillcoaching.co.uk